WE KNEW
William
Tecumseh
Sherman

Richard Wheeler

Thomas Y. Crowell Company
New York
Established 1834

LIBRARY OF CONGRESS CATALOGING IN PUBLICATION DATA

Wheeler, Richard.
  We knew William Tecumseh Sherman.

  Bibliography: p.
  Includes index.
    1. Sherman, William Tecumseh, 1820–1891. 2. United
States—History—Civil War, 1861–1865—Campaigns and
battles. 3. Generals—United States—Biography.
4. United States. Army—Biography. I. Title.
E467.1.S55W48   973.7'41 [B]   77-4334

ISBN 0-690-01426-0

10 9 8 7 6 5 4 3 2 1

To my mother, MARGARET WENRICH WHEELER,
who surprised me by recalling the words and tune
of "Sherman's March to the Sea" as it was sung
at her family's hearth nearly seventy years ago.

By Richard Wheeler

Voices of 1776
Voices of the Civil War
We Knew Stonewall Jackson
We Knew William Tecumseh Sherman

Preface

We Knew William Tecumseh Sherman is intended to be a companion book to the author's previous work, *We Knew Stonewall Jackson.* Jackson was right-hand man to General Robert E. Lee; Sherman was the same to General Ulysses S. Grant. A selection of people who knew Sherman and recorded their impressions have been brought together to help the author present a new account of the general's life. Many of the contributions are from sources long out of print, some now quite rare. The illustrations are by artists and engravers of Sherman's times.

Contents

Illustrations

Maps

ᵉ⁓I.

The Years Before
the Civil War

ᵉ⁓ *W*_{hen} *their sixth baby, a redheaded boy, was born to Charles
and Mary Sherman of Lancaster, Ohio, on February 8, 1820, he was
named after the Indian chief Tecumseh.*

*Prominent in Ohio's frontier history, Tecumseh had been known for
his wisdom and humanity. He was slain by American soldiers while
siding with the British during the War of 1812. Enemy or not, Charles
Sherman considered the chief a great man, and he convinced his wife
that the name was a fine one. Soon, however, everyone was calling
Tecumseh's little namesake simply "Cump."*

*During Cump's early years, Lancaster was a town of about 200
dwellings, with the Shermans living in a two-story frame house on
Main Street. Charles Sherman, after spending a dozen years as a frontier attorney and, part of this time, as Collector of Internal Revenue for
the Third Ohio District, had become a judge of the Ohio Supreme Court.
He wasn't wealthy, but he enjoyed a statewide reputation for integrity
and competence.*

*Sherman's best friend was Thomas Ewing, a prosperous attorney and
businessman who lived in a mansion a half block away. Ewing and his
wife Maria, like Charles and Mary Sherman, were abundantly en-
dowed with offspring. The two families were so close that the children
were almost interchangeable.*

*But Cump was only nine years old when the congenial circle was hit
by tragedy; Judge Sherman died. Mary was left with eleven young
Shermans. Thomas Ewing, feeling he had to do something to help,*

1

SHERMAN'S BIRTHPLACE in Lancaster, Ohio. Rear view. From a sketch made in 1865.

decided to take one of the boys into his home. Cump was picked because he was considered to be the brightest.

Otherwise, Ewing noted:

There was nothing specially remarkable about him, except that I never knew so young a boy who would do an errand so correctly and promptly as he did. He was transparently honest, faithful, and reliable. . . .

Maria Ewing gave the boy an affectionate welcome, and he became very fond of both his foster parents. The Ewing children treated him like a true brother. But Thomas Ewing noticed that Cump was "not quite at home." The trouble was that the boy was well aware he was an object of charity, and this bothered him. For the most part, however, he was content enough—especially since he could run down the block to his old home whenever he chose.

Learning that Cump had never been baptized, Maria Ewing asked Mary Sherman's permission to have it done by a Roman Catholic priest who paid monthly visits to the town. Though the Shermans were Presbyterians, Mary consented. The priest, surprised to find that the boy had been named after an Indian, declared, "He must have a Christian name as well." Since it happened to be Saint William's Day, the name was borrowed. Thus it was that the boy became William Tecumseh Sherman.

Cump lived up to his reputation for brightness, and his educational progress was excellent. Along with his younger brother John and other Sherman and Ewing children, the boy attended the Lancaster Academy. Here he came under the influence of Professor Samuel L. Howe, whom he was later to call "one of the best teachers in the United States."

Relates the professor's son, Warrington Howe:

My father ... was especially devoted to the inculcation of moral principle ... in the minds of his pupils.... And when love failed to accomplish the work, then physical discipline was called in.

Now the Sherman boys were proud, high-spirited fellows, like most American lads, and often wanted their own way.... Being duly informed [of their transgressions], the widow Sherman attended the college in person and said the proper correction should be administered under her own eye—and it was thus given.... Here was [Cump] Sherman's first great... lesson in discipline....

At home, according to Thomas Ewing, Cump was "correct in his habits." But this did not include an attention to the way he dressed. In spite of Maria Ewing's best efforts, he often looked shabby.

Hating his red hair (for in those days this color was an object of derision among the young), the boy once tried to dye it. It came up an odd shade of green that took months to grow out, and thereafter he submitted to being a redhead.

Cump lived the normal boyhood of the times and the region. When not in school or involved in family activities, he played games on the town's vacant lots or roamed the surrounding fields and woods. He and his chums hunted, fished, and gathered nuts and berries in season. A favorite visiting place was a farm owned by Aunt Sarah Clark, a sister to Thomas Ewing.

Phil Ewing, a foster brother his own age, was Cump's best friend. Often present—and at times in the way—was an admirer of the pair: a lively, intelligent, dark-haired girl four years younger, Cump's foster sister Ellen.

The boy went to work for the first time when he was fourteen. As a surveyor's rodman, he helped to lay out a waterway that connected Lancaster with the Ohio Canal. He was paid fifty cents a day.

During the summer of 1835, when Cump was fifteen, his younger brother John returned to Lancaster after living four years with a relative in Mount Vernon, Ohio, fifty miles away. John, who was destined for a long and distinguished career in national politics, says of his reunion with Cump:

My brother ... was three years my senior, and he and his associates of his own age rather looked down upon their juniors. Still, I had a good deal of intercourse with him, mainly in the way of advice on his part.

At that time he was a steady student, quiet in his manners, and easily moved by sympathy or affection. I was regarded as a wild, reckless lad, eager in controversy and ready to fight. No one could then anticipate that he was to be a great warrior and I a plodding lawyer and politician.

I fired my first gun over his shoulder. He took me with him to carry the game, mostly squirrels and pigeons. He was then destined to West Point, and was preparing for it.

Cump's cadetship at West Point was arranged by his foster father, who had become a United States Senator. The youth took the stagecoach east, detouring to Washington to pay Senator Ewing a visit. A thrilling hour was spent in peering through the White House fence, watching President Andrew Jackson pace the grounds. On his trip northward, Cump visited in New York City and attended a play starring Junius Brutus Booth. A steamboat took him up the Hudson River to the institute.

In an atmosphere of the strictest discipline, Cadet Sherman—sixteen years old, filled with nervous energy, wearing a gray uniform—began a four-year course that included both military and collegiate studies. Though he found it fairly easy to master all the components of the course, being equally at home on the drillfield and in the classroom, he had trouble sacrificing his individuality to the discipline. His success at the studies and exercises, however, gave him confidence, and it wasn't long before he lost the quiet demeanor he had arrived with. His true nature was revealed to be one of outspoken independence.

Among those who knew him at the institute was William S. Rosecrans, later a Union general:

Sherman was two classes above me, but he was one of the most popular and brightest fellows in the academy ... a bright-eyed, redheaded fellow who was always prepared for a lark of any kind, and who usually had grease spots on his pants. These spots came from our clandestine midnight feasts, at

ULYSSES S. GRANT.

which Sherman usually made the hash. He was considered the best hash maker at West Point ... a great honor.

The food given the cadets ... was furnished by contract. It was cheap and poor, and I sometimes think that the only meals we relished were our midnight hash lunches. We prepared for them by slipping boiled potatoes into our handkerchiefs when at the table, and hiding these away inside our vests. One of us would steal a lump of butter during a meal. ... In addition to this we would steal a little bit of bread, and some of the boys had in some way or another got hold of stewpans.

After the materials were gotten, one of the boys who had a retired room where there was least danger of discovery would whisper invitations to the rest to meet him that night for a hash feast. When we got there Sherman would mash the potatoes and mix them with pepper, salt and butter in such a way as to make a most appetizing dish. This he would cook in the stewpan over the fire [in the fireplace] ... and when it was done we would eat it sizzling hot on our bread, which we had toasted.

As we did so we would tell stories and have a jolly good time, and Sherman was one of the best storytellers of the lot. He was by no means a goody-goody boy, and he was one of those fellows who used to go down to Benny Haven's of a dark night, at the risk of expulsion, to eat oysters and drink beer. ...

Sherman... was very high in mathematics. He could have taken the honors, but... he was blunt in his ways. He had no policy or diplomacy about him, and if one of the professors asked him to do a problem, he would blurt out at times, "I can't do it."

"Why?" the professor would ask.

"Well, sir, to be frank with you, I haven't studied it."

Nevertheless, he stood so well as an honest, bright student that he was never punished for such remarks. But his carelessness, of course, cut down his average.

Numerous young men who were to make names for themselves during the Civil War attended the institute during Sherman's years there. Among them was Ulysses S. Grant, destined to be closely associated with Sherman on the battlefield but now separated from him by the institute's caste system. Grant began his first year as Sherman began his last.

Cump's foster sister Ellen had been writing to him all the while, not quite approving of the direction his life was taking. She would have preferred that he enter upon a profession that would enable him to stay close to home. Knowing that she favored the law, Cump wrote her:

I would rather be a blacksmith. Indeed, the nearer we come to... graduation day, the higher opinion I conceive of the duties and life of an officer of the United States Army, and the more confirmed in the wish of spending my life in the service of my country. Think of that!

In its earliest days, Sherman's class had numbered 115. By the last year this number had been reduced to forty-three, all the rest having failed to measure up. On graduation day, July 1, 1840, Sherman stood sixth in the class. He should have been fourth, but the number of demerits on his record had dragged him down.

Now twenty years old, Sherman was made a second lieutenant of artillery. Given a furlough before being assigned to a post, he returned to Lancaster to visit his relatives and friends.

Though Cump had drawn ever closer to his foster parents through the years, he had not forgotten his true mother, now living fairly comfortably with her three youngest children, part of her income gleaned from keeping boarders. Cump was to contribute to her support, as his own circumstances permitted, until her death in 1852.

Ellen Ewing, at sixteen years of age, found Cump a handsome sight in his uniform. Resigning herself to the fact that he planned to seek his success in distant places, she could only wish him the best of fortune.

But in its early years Sherman's military career failed to prosper. It brought him many novel experiences and adventures but no distinction and no advancement to the grades of higher pay. He was first assigned to Florida, where he spent about a year and a half, taking part in some minor expeditions against the Seminole Indians. His next post was Fort Morgan, in Mobile Bay, Alabama, where he served three months of garrison duty.

The summer of 1842 found Sherman at Fort Moultrie, in the harbor of Charleston, South Carolina. Fort Sumter, to become so famous later, was then only in the process of construction. Sherman spent several years at this post, taking part in Charleston's aristocratic social life and gaining a deep regard for the South and its people. Viewing slavery as essential to the Southern economy, he saw no point in weighing its morality.

For a time during his Charleston tour, Sherman took up art, writing Ellen:

I have great love for painting, and find that I am so fascinated that it amounts to pain to lay down the brush, placing me in doubt whether I had better stop it now, before it swallows all attention.

It was during the Charleston years that Cump and Ellen decided they would eventually marry.

In 1846, the first year of the Mexican War, Sherman was assigned to duty with an artillery company destined for California. Leaving New York Harbor on a government storeship, he began the long trip around Cape Horn, the southern tip of South America. An unnamed shipmate later described Sherman as

. . . a tall, spare man . . . with sandy hair and whiskers, and a reddish complexion. Grave in his demeanor, erect and soldierly in his bearing, he was especially noticeable for the faded and threadbare appearance of his uniform. . . . He was characterized . . . by entire devotion to his profession in all its details. His care for both the comfort and discipline of his men was constant and unwearied.

The voyage took 198 days, the vessel finally dropping anchor in Monterey Bay, California. Sherman went ashore with high hopes of achieving military glory, but he found himself in one of the war's quiet zones. There were no Mexicans to fight, and he had to settle for occupational duties.

Eighteen months later he wrote Ellen:

I have felt tempted to send my resignation to Washington, and I feel ashamed to wear epaulettes after having passed through a war without smelling gunpowder. But God knows I couldn't help it, so I'll let things pass.

Sherman spent three years in California. Memorably, he met the famous frontiersman Kit Carson. More memorably, he played a leading role in the army's investigation of the discovery of gold at John Sutter's sawmill in the Sacramento Valley. As the writer of the report to Washington that President James Polk used to announce the discovery to the world, Sherman had a hand in starting the great gold rush of 1849.

Returning to the East in 1850, Cump found his foster father famous in Washington circles. He was serving as Secretary of the Interior under the new President, Zachary Taylor. The Ewing family, lately of Lancaster, Ohio, was living in Blair House on Pennsylvania Avenue, not far from the White House.

On May 1 of that year, Cump Sherman and Ellen Ewing were married. He was thirty, she twenty-six. Despite his Catholic baptism, Cump was not a member of the church (he had grown up without embracing any particular creed), so Ellen had to settle for less than a full Catholic wedding. But it was a brilliant affair. Among the guests were President Taylor, his cabinet, and many other notables, including those two aging principals of the slavery issue, Senators Daniel Webster of Massachusetts and Henry Clay of Kentucky.

When the President took her hand to congratulate her, Ellen grew excited and leaned over and kissed him on the cheek. She told Cump later: "I didn't know what I was doing!"

With Ellen as his wife, Cump's spirits soared. His outlook was: "The present is ours. Let's make the most of it." Before the wedding, he had put in writing:

I publicly assume the high trust of your guardian and master.... You shall be my adjutant and chief counsellor.... Only be contented, happy, and repose proper trust in me....

It was now ten years since Sherman had left West Point, and that autumn he was finally promoted to captain. But the pay raise was insubstantial. For two more years he served the flag, a commissary officer at Saint Louis and New Orleans. Then he decided to try something else.

Departing the army (first by leave of absence, later by resignation), he became a banker, operating both in San Francisco and New York City.

He was an excellent banker, hardworking and resolutely honest. But the times were against him. His career ended, after four years, with the panic of 1857, and along with his career went his personal real-estate holdings and other investments. A good part of his assets went to military friends who had given him money to speculate with, money he felt obliged to pay back even though he was not legally bound to do so.

By this time Cump and Ellen had four children, two boys and two girls. To keep a roof over the family, Cump had to ask a loan of Thomas Ewing. This was freely given, but Cump's pride was deeply wounded.

While closing out some business in Saint Lous in the autumn of the panic year, Sherman was one day walking the sidewalk in the heaviest gloom when he saw a shabbily dressed man whose face he seemed to recall from the days at West Point. It was Ulysses S. Grant, whose own fortunes had declined. Sherman learned that he was selling firewood to help support his family, who lived on a farm near town. They talked for a time, then parted, having no reason to believe they would ever see each other again—those two failures, Ulysses S. Grant and William Tecumseh Sherman.

Sherman had once said that he would rather be a blacksmith than a lawyer, but he now became a lawyer. He joined a firm being set up in the frontier town of Leavenworth, Kansas, by two of Thomas Ewing's sons, Hugh and Tom, Jr., a firm which would soon include a fourth partner, Daniel McCook. Sherman, who had read some books on law during his years as a soldier and a banker, was admitted to the Kansas bar on the basis of "general knowledge and reputation."

According to a writer for the Leavenworth Conservative, *the new firm was established on the second floor of one of the town's most dilapidated frame buildings:*

The rooms . . . were reached by a crazy looking stairway on the outside, up which none ever went without dread of their falling. Dingy signs informed the curious that within was a "law shop" kept by . . . Ewing, Sherman & McCook. All were comparatively young men. All were ambitious. . . .

W. T. Sherman never mingled in our public affairs. . . . His neighbors tell of his abrupt manner, reserved yet forcible speech and character. . . .

While in the practice of law here, Sherman was consulting partner, having an almost insurmountable objection to pleading in court . . . [even though he had] a thorough knowledge of legal principles [and] a clear, logical perception of the points of equity involved in any case. He could present his views in the most direct manner, stripped of all verbiage, yet perfectly accurate in form. . . .

[One day] Sherman was compelled to appear before the Probate Judge. . . . The other partners were busy, and Sherman, with his authorities and the case all mapped out, proceeded to court.

He returned in a rage two hours after. . . . He had been pettifogged out of [winning] the case by a sharp, petty attorney opposed to him, in a way which was disgusting to his intellect and his convictions. . . . He swore that he would have nothing more to do with the law in this State. . . .

He sphered himself to our perception as the most remarkable intellectual embodiment of force it had been our fortune to encounter. . . . His eyes have an introverted look, but full of smoldering fire. . . . His temperament is nervous-sanguine, and he is full of crochets and prejudices, which, however, never stand in the way of practical results. The idea, or rather object, which rules him, for the time, overrides everything else. Round the mouth [however, is] . . . a gleam of saturnine humor. . . .

As Sherman's interest in a law career waned, he threw himself into another project. His foster father owned a large farm about forty miles from Leavenworth, and Sherman undertook its management. Believing that a great market for corn was about to develop, since more and more pioneers were passing through Kansas on their way westward, he secured Ewing's permission to buy 5,000 bushels of corn on speculation. His luck ran true to form: the market never developed.

Ellen, who was soon to have another child, was in Lancaster, Ohio, at this time. Cump wrote her:

I am doomed to be a vagabond, and shall no longer struggle against my fate. . . . I look upon myself as a dead cock in the pit, not worthy of further notice, and will take my chances as they come.

During this period, Cump often visited in Leavenworth with Tom Ewing, Jr. Tom's wife, Ellie, considered Cump a superb conversationalist, even though his mood made him especially sharp-tongued.

In the words of Tom Ewing III:

Once she had as guests several clergymen who were attending a Presbyterian meeting in town. . . . One of them remarked that swearing was a wholly unnecessary and inexcusable vice.

He snapped out, "Were you ever at sea in a heavy gale, with spars creaking and sails flapping, and the crew cowardly and incompetent?"

"No."

"Did you ever drive a five-team ox-cart across the prairie?"

"No."

"Then you know nothing of the temptations to blasphemy. You are not competent to judge."

In August, 1859, two new opportunities came Sherman's way at the same time. A group of Cincinnati financiers asked him to become their representative in London, and the State of Louisiana wanted his aid with the establishment of a new military college, over which he was to become superintendent. He decided upon the post in Louisiana.

At first Sherman was content with his choice. It offered him not only a decent salary but, as he put it, "solitude and banishment enough to hide from the misfortunes of the past." He went to Louisiana alone, planning to send for his wife and five children after he built them a new house. He soon had the school in operation, and was well liked by both the staff and the cadets. According to one of the cadets, Sherman was a supervisor who "knew how to reprimand" but also knew the importance of "words of kindness and encouragement." Though the job had its vexations and complications, they were successfully mastered.

But the Civil War was now at hand. Though Sherman was not against slavery, deeming it a practical necessity, and though he had an abiding affection for the South, he was a strong Union man. When Louisiana seceded in January, 1861, becoming the sixth state to do so, Sherman, spurning all pleas that he stay on at the school, resigned and went north.

Whitelaw Reid, a newspaperman of Sherman's home state, was later to explain:

He was now in his forty-second year.... His thirteen years of army life had brought him no distinction.... The eight years of civil life that followed had added little to his fortune and nothing to his fame.... But the heart of the man was sound to the core, and his... abandonment of his place in Louisiana did more than all his life thus far to fix him in men's minds.

~II.

First Bull Run
to Paducah

~*Sherman arrived back in the North in early March, 1861. One of the first things he did was to go to Washington and see his brother John, who was now a Senator from Ohio.*

In John's words:

He was deeply impressed with the certainty of war and of its magnitude, and was impelled by the patriotic sentiment that, as he had been educated at the expense of the government for military service, it was his duty, in the then condition of the country, to tender his services. I therefore escorted him to the White House.... Mr. Lincoln ... in response to his tender ... expressed a hope ... that the danger would pass by and that the Union would be restored by a peaceful compromise.

As it became clear to Sherman that his offer was being refused, he grew angry but held his tongue. Once outside the White House, however, he snapped at his brother, "You politicians have got things in a hell of a fix, and you may get them out as best you can." He added that the country was sleeping on a volcano which might erupt at any minute, but that he was going to ignore the whole matter and look to the care of his family. Ellen, incidentally, was pregnant again.

Cump at once took a job as president of a street railway company in Saint Louis. He and Ellen were barely established in their new home before Washington offered Cump a chance to become assistant Secretary

12

ABRAHAM LINCOLN.

of War. He declined, wishing the Administration "all success in its almost impossible task of governing this distracted and anarchical people."

A few days later, on April 12, the Confederates opened their guns on Fort Sumter, in Charleston Harbor. The Federals in the fort surrendered the next day. On April 15, with North and South alike in a state of wild excitement, Lincoln called for 75,000 militia volunteers to serve against the rebellion for three months.

Even now, Sherman refused requests for his help. According to a friend who discussed the matter with him:

He declared it would be as wise to undertake to extinguish the flames of a burning building with a squirt gun as to put down the rebellion with three months' troops. His plan was to organize for a gigantic war, to call out the whole military power of the country at once, and, by the exercise of irresistible force, to crush the rebellion in its incipiency.

President Lincoln himself soon realized he would have to do more than ask the states to send him short-term militiamen. In early May he called for 42,000 three-year volunteers and directed that the regular army and the navy be enlarged. This made a little more sense to Sherman, and he now offered his services, accepting the rank of colonel in the regular army.

While his troops were being recruited, Sherman paid a visit to Williamsport, Maryland, where his brother John was serving temporarily on the staff of General Robert Patterson, commander of the forces in that area. John says that Cump found him with a group of officers at a country tavern:

He then met, for the first time in many years, his old [West Point] classmate . . . George H. Thomas, who then commanded a regular regiment of the United States Army in the force under the command of General Patterson.

The conversation of these two officers, who were to be so intimately associated in great events in the future, was very interesting. They got a big map of the United States, spread it on the floor, and on their hands and knees discussed the probable salient strategic places of the war. They singled out Richmond, Vicksburg, Nashville, Knoxville and Chattanooga.

To me it has always appeared strange that they were able confidently and correctly to designate the lines of operations and strategic points of a war not yet commenced, and more strange still that they should be leading actors in great battles at the places designated by them at this country tavern.

At the time of the map incident, however, Sherman had little faith in the war's outcome or in his own future. He saw himself as a man with a large family to support in a nation headed for ruin.

At the nation's capital, where the main army was forming under General Irvin McDowell, Sherman took charge of a brigade composed of five regiments, four from New York and one from Wisconsin. These recruits had a great enthusiasm for their crusade to save the Union, but Sherman saw them as being woefully unaware of what they were up against. Figuring they might well stampede at the first sound of gunfire, he was annoyed by their confident cries of "On to Richmond!" While trying to instruct them in the military fundamentals in the short time the situation allowed, he showed them little patience.

All in all, Sherman reacted badly to the national crisis. It is true that he was one of the very few leaders to grasp its dimensions, but his vision was dominated by acute pessimism. As a result, he now entered a long period marked by spells of depression and irritability.

RECRUITS from New York in a camp near Washington.

The premature march of the army toward Richmond in mid-July (only three months after the fall of Fort Sumter) did nothing to help Sherman's outlook. The army proceeded by way of Manassas Junction, about twenty-five miles southwest of Washington, where the Confederates waited. As the raw volunteers swung along in the highest spirits, followed by crowds of civilians who believed they were about to witness a quick end to the rebellion, Colonel Sherman predicted to those who would listen that this movement was but the start of a long war.

Sherman underwent his baptism of fire in a preliminary skirmish, saying later:

At Blackburn's Ford ... for the first time in my life I saw cannonballs strike men and crash through the trees and saplings above and around us. ...

The main event, the Battle of First Bull Run, or Manassas, occurred on Sunday, July 21, with the Confederate army being commanded by Generals Joseph E. Johnston and Pierre G. T. Beauregard. Colonel Sherman was under fire about four hours; he was twice grazed, and his horse was wounded. According to a newspaper correspondent, "His

Joseph E. Johnston.

coolness and efficiency surprised friends familiar with his excitable temperament."

Sherman's men fought better than he thought they would. In the end, however, they retreated, along with the rest of the army, leaving the field to the Southerners. This was the day on which Confederate General Thomas Jonathan Jackson earned the sobriquet "Stonewall."

Sherman was totally disgusted by the nature of the retreat. The army, mingled with the civilian spectators, swarmed back toward Washington in great disorder, some of the men in a state of panic—this even though the Confederates were not pursuing. Reacting profanely, Sherman did what he could to alleviate the chaos.

Relates William T. Lusk, a New Yorker with Sherman's brigade:

On our return to Fort Corcoran after the battle, having walked over thirty miles from the battlefield, having been thirty-six hours without food or sleep, consequently exhausted from fatigue, hunger, and want of rest, we hoped to be allowed to throw ourselves anywhere, and to get a mouthful of anything to eat. The rain poured in torrents and we were soaked to our skins. There was not a cracker to be had . . . not a tent to shelter us. We crawled into an old barn.

Sherman . . . [having decided to put some horses into the

PIERRE G. T. BEAUREGARD.

AN INCIDENT of the Union retreat from First Bull Run as conceived by a studio artist.

barn] ordered us to come out.... Many of the men were desperate. They became clamorous for food. Sherman sneered at
them for such unsoldierly conduct. They begged for some
place to rest. He bade them sleep on the ground. They had no
blankets, many not even a jacket, and all were shivering in the
wet. The soil was oozy with water, and deep puddles lay
everywhere. The men became querulous. Sherman grew angry,
called them a pack of New York loafers and thieves.

*A day or two later some of the three-month volunteers, in a mutinous
mood, demanded their discharges. Though they had served their time,
Sherman as yet had no authority to release them. Ordering some artillery
pieces unlimbered, he vowed to open fire on the men if they tried to leave
camp. This ended the trouble.*

*On a succeeding morning Sherman was approached by a young
officer who said that he intended to leave camp that day, discharge or
not. "If you attempt it," warned Sherman, touching his breast as though
assuring himself that he had his pistol under his coat, "I will shoot you
like a dog!" The officer decided not to attempt it.*

*That same day President Lincoln paid a visit to Sherman and his
troops. The President was pleased at the order, cleanliness, and discipline he found, but the dissatisfaction in the ranks was evident. The
unhappy young officer came forward and said, "Mr. President, I have
a grievance. Colonel Sherman has threatened to shoot me."*

*Lincoln, figuring that Sherman knew his own business best, replied,
"Well, if I were you, and he threatened to shoot, I would not trust him,
for I believe he would do it."*

*The troops began to laugh, and the young officer slipped away.
Thereafter it was easier for Sherman to maintain discipline.*

*In the words of Colonel S. M. Bowman, who not only served in the
war with Sherman but became the author of a book on his campaigns:*

The sharpness with which Colonel Sherman criticized the
conduct of some of the officers and men of his brigade at Bull
Run, both in his official report and in his free conversations,
made him many enemies; but the vigor he had displayed on the
field, added to the influence of his brother, the Honorable
John Sherman, led the Ohio delegation in Congress to recom-
mend his promotion.

He was commissioned as a Brigadier-General of Volunteers
on the 3d of August, 1861.... For a short time after this he had
command of a brigade in the Army of the Potomac, but early in

September, upon the organization of the Department of Kentucky, he was transferred to that theatre of operations, and ordered to report, as second in command, to Brigadier-General Robert Anderson, who was placed at the head of the department.

Kentucky was one of the war's border states. Lying between the Union and the Confederacy, its sympathies were divided. General Anderson, then headquartered at Louisville, on Kentucky's north central border, was responsible for keeping the state in the Union. This threatened to be a difficult task, since Anderson had but few troops. Fortunately for the Union cause, the Confederate forces, operating from Tennessee, just south of Kentucky, were also low in numbers at this stage of the war.

Sherman was shortly sent to Muldraugh's Hill, south of Louisville, where he commanded about 3,000 men in a defensive position. Mistakenly believing that the Confederates, who had entered southern Kentucky, were very strong, he expected a determined advance to develop, and he was surprised when none did. Fresh troops kept reaching his camp, but only in small numbers.

According to one of his officers, Colonel R. M. Kelly:

General Sherman's army was rather a motley crew. The Home Guards did not wear regulation uniforms, and . . . [the Federal volunteers] were not well equipped. . . .

Sherman's attention was attracted to a young man without any uniform who was moving around with what he considered suspicious activity, and he called him up for question. The young fellow gave a prompt account of himself. His name was Griffiths, he was a medical student from Louisville acting as hospital steward, and he had been called out in such a hurry that he had had no time to get his uniform.

As he moved away he muttered something in a low tone to an officer standing by, and Sherman at once demanded to know what it was.

"Well, General," was the [officer's] reply, "he said that a general with such a hat as you have on had no right to talk to him about a uniform."

Sherman was wearing a battered hat of the style known as "stovepipe." Pulling it off, he looked at it, and, bursting into a laugh, called out: "Young man, you are right about the hat, but you ought to have your uniform."

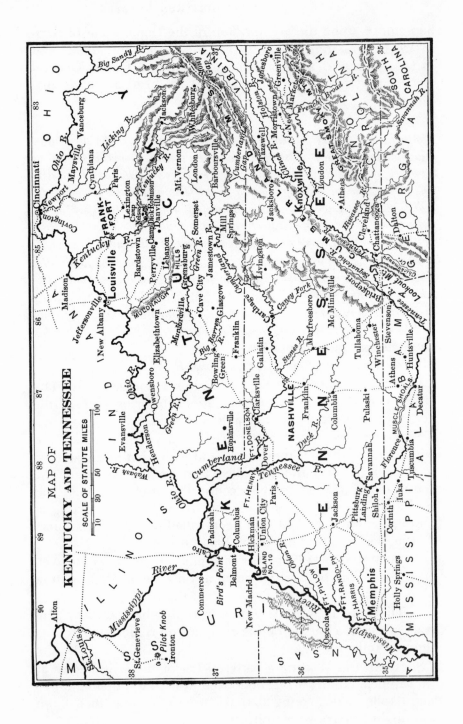

MAP OF
KENTUCKY AND TENNESSEE

SCALE OF STATUTE MILES
10 30 50 100

*This was an exceptional instance of humor in a most difficult period of
Sherman's career. He was becoming more and more depressed over the
Union's chances for survival, and he got the idea that Kentucky was as
good as lost and that he was facing ruin as an officer. Matters were
greatly worsened when General Anderson, because of his own "mental
torture," quit his post on October 8 and left Sherman in top command.*

*Operating from department headquarters in Louisville, Sherman
came under the critical observation of the town's war correspondents.
He was not popular with the press, making a practice of telling correspondents bluntly that they published too much information that gave
aid to the enemy. He placed restrictions on their news gathering, and he
once jailed a correspondent who disobeyed him.*

*In Louisville, Sherman lived on the ground floor of a hotel called the
Galt House, and one correspondent soon noted that*

. . . he paced the corridor outside his rooms for hours, absorbed. The guests whispered about him. . . . He spoke with
unwise vehemence of . . . the military situation in Kentucky. . . .
He was simply appalled by the difficulties . . . and could not rid
himself of the apprehension that he was due for defeat if the
rebels attacked.

*On October 16, Secretary of War Simon Cameron, while on a trip
through the war's western theater for President Lincoln, met with Sherman in his rooms at the Galt House. One of the officers present was
Brigadier General Thomas J. Wood, who tells what took place:*

Mr. Cameron . . . asked General Sherman what his plans
were. To this General Sherman replied that he had no
plans. . . . To resist an advance of the rebels, General Sherman
stated that he did not have at that time in Kentucky more than
some twelve to fourteen thousand effective men. . . .

Having explained the situation from the defensive point of
view, General Sherman proceeded to consider it from the offensive standpoint. . . . For the purpose of expelling the rebels
from Kentucky, General Sherman said that at least sixty
thousand soldiers were necessary. . . .

General Sherman expressed the opinion that, to carry the
war to the Gulf of Mexico and destroy all armed opposition to
the Government in the entire Mississippi Valley at least two
hundred thousand troops were absolutely requisite.

[Other witnesses got the impression that Sherman wanted
200,000 men for the work in Kentucky alone, that he quoted

60,000 as the number he needed just to hold the foe at bay, and that he said he would need an extra 140,000 in order to take the offensive.]

... Mr. Cameron asked, with much warmth and apparent irritation, "Where do you suppose, General Sherman, all this force is to come from?" General Sherman replied that he did not know; that it was not his duty to raise, organize, and put the necessary military force into the field; that duty pertained to the War Department. His duty was to organize campaigns and command the troops after they had been put into the field. ...

A short time after the council was held ... an imperfect narrative of it appeared in the New York *Tribune*. This account announced to the public the conclusions uttered by General Sherman in the council [making them seem absurd], without giving the reasons on which his conclusions were based.

Had Sherman withheld his views on numbers for a few months, they would have caused less of a stir. The armies in the West, both Union and Confederate, were to begin growing in a way that hadn't been foreseen at the war's inception.

But there is no doubt that Sherman's judgment was seriously impaired during this period. He soon asked to be relieved of his command, at the same time writing Ellen, then in Lancaster, Ohio, that his worries had him "almost crazy." Both his wife and his brother the Senator came to Louisville to soothe and encourage Cump, and they did not leave until he seemed to be considerably improved.

Replaced by Brigadier General Don Carlos Buell in mid-November, Sherman was assigned to the Department of Missouri, farther to the west. He reported to Saint Louis for duty under a friend from his days at West Point and his service in California, Major General Henry W. Halleck.

In spite of what the newspapers were saying about Sherman, Halleck assigned him to duty in the field. But this failed to work out. Sherman quickly began to worry as he had in Kentucky and could think only in defensive terms. Halleck was forced to recall him to Saint Louis.

One of the town's war correspondents noted that Sherman smoked cigars excessively and that

... his eye had a half-wild expression. ... He sleeps little. Nor do the most powerful opiates relieve his terrible cerebral excitement.

Henry W. Halleck.

According to another correspondent:

The General . . . spoke despondingly; said the rebels could never be whipped; talked of a thirty years' war.

Ellen Sherman, now deeply agitated over Cump's condition, came to Saint Louis. Ellen's lot was unenviable. By the time the war broke out she had been married to Cump for eleven years, and their life together—and apart—had never run smoothly for more than a few months at a time. Cump's showing at Bull Run convinced Ellen he had finally found the career he was intended for, that he would soon become one of the heroes of the times. Ellen's new disappointment was a bitter one. As before, however, her loyalty and devotion to her husband remained unshaken. She even kept her faith in his potential, believing that he would yet "win laurels inferior to no man's."

But Cump's friend and commanding officer, Henry Halleck, was obliged to report to Washington on December 2:

General Sherman's physical and mental system is so completely broken by labor and care as to render him for the present entirely unfit for duty. Perhaps a few weeks' rest may restore him. I am satisfied that in his present condition it would be dangerous to give him a command here.

Cump was granted a twenty-day leave of absence, and Ellen took him to a house she had rented near the Ewing mansion in Lancaster. Cump was not only tired and disconsolate but also filled with regret over the anguish he was causing the Ewings and his brother John, none of whom had ever stopped believing in him. This was their gravest trial.

The situation quickly worsened. On December 11, the Cincinnati Commercial *carried the following item:*

GENERAL WILLIAM T. SHERMAN INSANE

The painful intelligence reaches us, in such form that we are not at liberty to disclose it, that Gen. William T. Sherman . . . is insane. It appears that he was, at the time while commanding in Kentucky, stark mad. . . . He has of course been relieved altogether from command. The harsh criticisms that have been lavished on this gentleman, provoked by his strange conduct, will now give way to feelings of deepest sympathy for him in his great calamity.

This item, which was picked up and published nationally, put the Ewing family and John Sherman into an uproar. Phil Ewing, the chum of Cump's childhood, hurried to Cincinnati and prodded the Commercial *into printing a denial composed by Cump and himself. Cump's foster father, Thomas Ewing, wrote from Washington that the "libelous scoundrels" ought to be sued.*

John Sherman went to see Lincoln and was able to report that the President had "the kindest feeling" for Cump and would welcome a visit from him. But Cump was too dispirited to go.

At no time during this ordeal did Cump and Ellen feel worse than on the day their son Tommy came running into the house saying that a boy in the street had told him, "Your papa is crazy."

Sherman's problem, of course, was not insanity but a critical lapse of self-confidence. This becomes understandable in the light of his record after leaving West Point. He had applied himself diligently to one pursuit after another but had never achieved a single solid success. Fortunately, he was surrounded by understanding people, many of them nationally prominent, who never tired of helping him—people who seemed to see in him a spark of genius he did not see himself.

The appearance of the news item marked the lowest point in Sherman's depression. From then on, he began to recover, though slowly at first. It was almost as though the item was the jolt he needed to put his thinking back on a rational course. He was soon able to see, for example, that he had exaggerated the strength of the enemy in the West. Though Ellen wanted him to remain in Lancaster until spring, Cump left on December 18 to report back to his friend Halleck in Saint Louis.

Cump soon wrote his brother John:

I am so sensible now of my disgrace from having exaggerated the force of our enemy . . . that I do think I should have committed suicide were it not for my children. I do not think I can again be entrusted with a command.

General Halleck assigned Sherman to training recruits. This grieved Ellen, who considered it an inferior assignment, "an endorsement of the slander." Going to Washington, Ellen joined her father for an evening visit with the President. He assured them, as he had assured John, that he liked Cump and added a profession of faith in his future as an officer.

It wasn't necessary for the President to intercede in this matter. General Halleck knew what he was doing. He gradually increased Sherman's responsibilities, which resulted in a corresponding increase in his confidence. By mid-February, 1862, Cump was in charge at Paducah, in western Kentucky. This was a rear-area supply depot for operations being conducted by Brigadier General Ulysses S. Grant to the southeast, on the Tennessee border.

Fort Henry, a Confederate post on the Tennessee River, had already fallen. And on February 16, after several days of fighting, the Confederates at Fort Donelson, on the Cumberland River, stilled their guns. The commander, General Simon B. Buckner, sent out a note in which he agreed to discuss terms. Grant wrote back:

No terms except an unconditional and immediate surrender can be accepted. I propose to move immediately upon your works.

Buckner capitulated, and U. S. Grant became "Unconditional Surrender" Grant in Northern newspapers. He had gained the Union's first important victory. Breaking the Confederate line that spanned southwestern Kentucky, he had opened the whole of western Tennessee to invasion.

While the South lamented, a wave of joy swept the North. Sherman, at the Paducah supply depot, was conscious of a heavy weight leaving his breast. There was hope for the Union after all. And there was also personal hope; he might well get a chance to redeem his good name.

General Grant had reason to be pleased with his communications with Sherman, saying later:

At that time he was my senior in rank, and there was no authority of law to assign a junior to command a senior of the same grade. But every boat that came up with supplies or reinforcements brought a note of encouragement from Sherman, asking me to call upon him for any assistance he could render and saying that if he could be of service at the front I might send for him and he would waive rank.

In the words of Federal war correspondent Albert D. Richardson, who knew both Grant and Sherman:

This unusual readiness to waive rank ... quite won Grant's heart, and was the beginning of a friendship like that of David and Jonathan. Under any superior, Sherman would have deserved well of the Republic; but it needed a nature like Grant's—large, generous, incapable of being disturbed by little ebullitions of impatience and arrogance—to make his pure patriotism and his splendid military genius known and seen by all men.

III.

Bloody Shiloh

*B*y *latter March, 1862, many Northerners were telling them-selves that the war was nearly over. The situation looked bright in both the eastern and western theaters. At Hampton Roads, Virginia, the world's first battle between two ironclad vessels had resulted in the neutralization of the South's* Merrimac *by the North's* Monitor; *this opened the way for a second advance upon Richmond, this one starting with a voyage down the Potomac River and Chesapeake Bay. In the West, two strong armies had pushed southward from Kentucky deep into western Tennessee.*

Grant was now a major general. At the beginning of April he was in command of about 42,000 men at Pittsburg Landing and nearby Crump's Landing, on the west bank of the Tennessee River, only a few miles from the northern border of Mississippi. Sherman, now nearly back to normal, was with him as a division commander. Marching from Columbia, Tennessee, eighty-five miles to the northeast, to join Grant was a part of the second army, 20,000 men under Don Carlos Buell.

The retreating Confederates had regrouped at Corinth, Mississippi, about twenty miles southwest of Grant's position. In strength they were about equal to Grant's army, without Buell. The Confederate com-mander was General Albert Sidney Johnston (not to be confused with Joseph E. Johnston, then commanding in the East). Second in command in the West was a newcomer, Pierre Beauregard of First Bull Run.

Johnston and Beauregard decided that their best chance against the

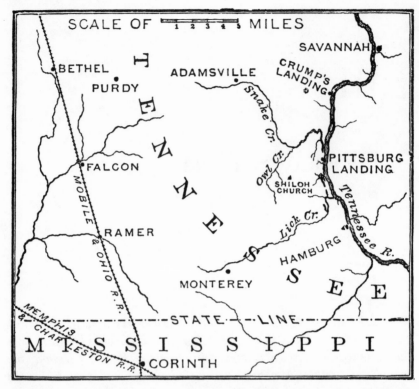

SCALE OF ⊢1 2 3 4 5⊣ MILES

SAVANNAH

BETHEL
PURDY

ADAMSVILLE

CRUMP'S
LANDING

TENNE

Snake Cr.

FALCON

Owl Cr.

PITTSBURG
LANDING

SHILOH
CHURCH

Tennessee R.

RAMER

Lick Cr.

MOBILE & OHIO R.R.

HAMBURG

MONTEREY

S E E

STATE LINE

MEMPHIS & CHARLESTON R.R.

M I S S I S S I P P I

CORINTH

OUTLINE MAP of Shiloh campaign. Confederates advanced from
Corinth (bottom of map) northeastward toward Shiloh Church where
Federal line, facing southwestward, stretched between Owl and Lick
creeks. On the battle's first day the Federals were driven back toward
Pittsburg Landing, finally holding at dusk. On the second day the
Federals, having been strongly reinforced during the night, coun-
terattacked and drove the Confederates from the field.

*Union forces in Tennessee lay in taking the offensive, and this without
delay. They would attack Grant before Buell arrived to reinforce him.
With Grant defeated, Buell could be attended to.*

*The Confederate plan had more in its favor than the two generals
realized. Underestimating their resolve, Grant saw no danger of his
being attacked at Pittsburg Landing while he awaited Buell. He figured
that the Confederates, after their recent defeats, would choose to remain
at Corinth and brace themselves for the next Union advance.*

*Grant's men were not entrenched. This early in the war neither side
was very security conscious. The Federals occupied tent camps scattered*

over a great undulating area of woods and fields in the vicinity of Shiloh Church, a simple log structure about two and a half miles inland from the river.

The divisions of Generals Sherman and Benjamin M. Prentiss formed the front line that faced toward Corinth. Sherman was on the right, his flank reaching toward Owl Creek, one of the river's tributaries. Three additional divisions were on the field, and one more was at Crump's Landing, a few miles to the north.

Unaware of the enemy's plans, Sherman was in good spirits as he busied himself around his camp. Wearing his battered stovepipe hat and puffing the inevitable cigar, he gave orders, dictated dispatches, and talked in his rapid way on many topics. According to one of his officers, "It would be easier to say what he did not talk about than what he did." His nervous energy never abating, Sherman often paced as he talked, toying with a button on his coat or scratching his chin through his close-cropped beard. Some of the troops eyed him suspiciously, a little dubious about serving under a man who had so recently been called insane.

By the evening of Saturday, April 5, the Confederates, with their infantry units, cavalrymen, artillery batteries, supply wagons, and ambulances, were forming battle lines within two miles of the Union camp. The leading troops had been spotted but were believed to be only a scouting party sent up from Corinth.

As related by Colonel Wills de Hass, of Sherman's division:

That evening a free interchange of opinion took place at our tent, where General Sherman called while we were at tea.... He was incredulous that an attack was meditated—believed they were only present to watch our movements; said news had been received that evening that Buell would join us in forty-eight hours, and then we would advance on Corinth. General Sherman's positive manner of uttering his opinions had the effect to quiet the apprehensions of some of the officers present, but others ... were convinced that attack was at hand....

How unconscious of danger lay the army of the Union that night! ... [The men's] visions were of home and the loved ones who looked so fondly for their return.... At midnight, stepping from my tent beneath the shadow of that quiet church, I listened for the premonition of the coming storm. But all was still save the measured tread of the sentinel and the gentle whispers of the genial night breeze. No sound came from the distant wood....

CONFEDERATES charging upon the Union camp.

Long before early dawn on that calm Sabbath morn the rebel army had breakfasted and stripped for the bloody work before them. Their blankets, knapsacks, etc., were laid aside, their only encumbrance being their arms, haversacks, and canteens. . . . By three o'clock they were on the move. . . .

[Grant's] troops, particularly the advance division under Sherman, were mostly fresh from the recruiting camps, and wholly unpracticed, even in the simplest company maneuvres. Many of the regiments were not supplied with arms until their departure [from Kentucky]. . . .

The Union camps had just begun to stir at dawn, with many of the men at their breakfast fires, when the Confederates opened fire on a patrol sent out from Prentiss's lines and on the pickets stationed out in front of Sherman. Wills de Hass was one of the first to learn from the pickets that the enemy was approaching in force, and he hurried to Sherman's headquarters tent, a few hundred yards to the rear:

. . . for some minutes we listened to the firing. The General appeared to be in doubt as to attack, but ordered the brigade into readiness for action. . . . The morning was bright, warm, and genial. . . . The woods were vocal with feathered songsters. . . . It was now about half-past six o'clock. The fire on our front grew hotter and nearer.

SHERMAN at Shiloh.

Soon the pickets came rushing back in dismay, some of them bleeding from wounds. As these men continued on toward the rear, many of the troops in the first line caught their panic and joined the flight.

Sherman still believed that no more than a large scouting party was near. He and his staff rode forward. As they stopped to train their glasses on the forest and its few open areas, some muskets cracked in a patch of bushes to their left-front, and Sherman's orderly dropped dead from the saddle.

Soon afterward Sherman noted that one of the thinner expanses of woods held a mass of Confederates stretching far to the rear. "My God," he cried, "we're attacked!" Swinging his horse around, he began a furious ride to prepare his units for heavy fighting.

By this time birds, squirrels, and rabbits, driven before the Confederates, were skittering among the Union tents. Wills de Hass was observing from a point near the log church:

... looking down into the dark wood from which issued the deep roar of heavy cannon and the sharp rattle of musketry, scarcely a man was visible; but as the unclouded sun fell on their burnished arms the whole scene became lighted up, presenting a panorama most effective. . . . The lines closed steadily on us, the enemy moving forward at all points.

The Confederates whooped wildly as they came, many shouting "Bull Run! Bull Run!" Some of the Federals said later that the attackers acted as though the canteens they paused to swig from held a mixture of whiskey and gunpowder.

Soon, says Wills de Hass, "the line near Sherman's headquarters was . . . driven back in confusion."

Sherman was busy trying to establish a stronger line a little farther to the rear. Jesse Bowman Young, a youthful soldier who had retreated on the run from the first line, was encouraged to find the general

. . . riding all along the ranks, stationing the infantry, putting the batteries into position, aiming the very guns with his own hands, seeming to be everywhere at once. Toward the rear, scenes of confusion and alarm were prevailing, but among the ranks about him . . . many . . . were cool and self-possessed. . . .

Young goes on to relate that a few moments later he was discussing the appalling situation with a mounted cavalry major when Sherman rode up and said:

"Major, give me some extra men for orderlies. One of mine has been shot already. Take the rest of your battalion down toward the Landing and drive back all the stragglers you can find. The devil's to pay, sure enough. Hundreds of men all around here have run without firing a gun. . . ."

And off the general galloped, his clothes torn and soiled, and his hand bleeding from a wound he had just received.

Adds war correspondent Whitelaw Reid:

Dashing along the lines, encouraging them everywhere by his presence and exposing his own life with the same freedom which he demanded their offer of theirs, he did much to save the division from utter destruction.

Prentiss's division had broken. Elements of General John A. McClernand's division were now supporting Sherman on the left. Farther back, the divisions of Generals W. H. L. Wallace and Stephen A. Hurlbut

UNION AMMUNITION WAGONS heading for the front as the wounded and the stragglers pass to the rear.

were forming for action. At Crump's Landing, northward along the rive, the division under General Lewis Wallace (later the author of Ben Hur) *was just preparing to start for the battlefield. Buell's army, completing its march from Columbia, was nearing the east bank of the river.*

General Grant, on the east bank waiting for Buell when the fighting began, had crossed over and was now at the front. He was suffering from an ankle injury acquired in a recent horseback accident, but this did not impede his effectiveness. According to war correspondent Albert Richardson:

At ten o'clock he rode to Sherman, whose gallantry and coolness deserved and received his enthusiastic praise.

"I fear we shall run out of cartridges," said Sherman.

"Oh," replied the chief, "I have provided for that."

Failure in this would have been failure in everything; but all day, over the narrow, crowded roads from the river, ammunition wagons . . . came promptly forward.

Grant rode over to the left. About eleven o'clock, Rowley [i.e.,

Captain William R. Rowley, one of Grant's aides], returning to Sherman, found him standing among his troops with his left hand resting on a tree, while he gazed eagerly forward toward the skirmishers.

Rowley: "General Grant sent me to see how you are getting along."

Sherman: "Tell him if he has any men to spare I can use them; if not, I will do the best I can. We are holding them pretty well just now . . . but it's as hot as hell."

Rowley, noticing a white handkerchief wrapped about Sherman's hand, asked: "Why, general, are you wounded?"

Sherman looked down wonderingly, as if he had just discovered it, and answered: "Well, yes. But that don't begin to hurt like this damned thing on my shoulder, which I suppose hasn't left any mark whatever."

A spent ball had struck his shoulder-strap. His horse, too, had been shot under him. But he was the animating spirit of the entire right-front and center. If he was insane, it was with the inspired madness of heroes and martyrs.

Sherman's efforts, and those of the other Union generals, were seriously hampered by the desertions from the ranks. Several thousand men had stampeded to the rear and were huddling under the bank of the river. But the generals under Johnston and Beauregard—William J. Hardee, Braxton Bragg, Leonidas Polk, and John C. Breckinridge—had problems too. Beauregard was to report later that many of the men "abandoned their colors . . . to pillage the captured encampments," and that others, coming under Union cannon and musket fire, "retired shamefully from the field."

But the thousands of men who remained at the front on both sides, though inexperienced in warfare, managed to make the battle a busy and brutal one. War correspondent Junius Henri Browne says that "the sound was deafening, the tumult indescribable."

The light of the sun was obscured by the clouds of sulphurous smoke. . . . Men with knitted brows and flushed cheeks fought madly . . . with blood and perspiration streaming down their faces. . . . Everywhere was mad excitement. . . . Captains, majors, colonels, and generals fought like private soldiers, and it was not uncommon to see a field officer firing a musket or charging with his revolver. . . . The paths were filled with the dying and the dead. . . . No life was worth a farthing. . . . Death was in the air, and bloomed like a poison plant on every foot of soil.

General Grant relates:

A number of attempts were made by the enemy to turn our right flank, where Sherman was posted, but every effort was repulsed with heavy loss. But the front attack was kept up so vigorously that, to prevent the success of these attempts to get on our flanks, the National troops were compelled, several times, to take positions to the rear, nearer Pittsburg Landing. . . .

At one of the spots on Grant's left where his troops put up a stout resistance stood a peach orchard in full bloom. The bullets and artillery missiles, along with the reverberating noises, caused the petals to fall like snow.

It was near the peach orchard that Confederate General Albert Sidney Johnston bled to death about two-thirty in the afternoon after taking a bullet in the leg. This was a sad blow to the entire Confederate cause, for Johnston was then considered to be the best general in the South.

Assuming the command in Johnston's place, Pierre Beauregard cried, "Forward, boys! Drive them into the river!"

Again in Grant's words:

In one of the backward moves . . . the division commanded by General Prentiss did not fall back with the others. This left his flanks exposed and enabled the enemy to capture him with about 2200 of his officers and men [the capture taking place at a bitterly contested spot the Confederates named the Hornet's Nest]. . . .

With the single exception of a few minutes after the capture of Prentiss, a continuous and unbroken line was maintained all day from . . . right to . . . left. . . .

There was no hour during the day when there was not heavy firing and generally hard fighting at some point on the line, but seldom at all points at the same time. It was a case of Southern dash against Northern pluck and endurance. . . .

. . . I was continuously engaged in passing from one part of the field to another, giving directions to division commanders. In thus moving along the line, however, I never deemed it important to stay long with Sherman. Although his troops were then under fire for the first time, their commander, by his constant presence with them, inspired a confidence in officers and men that enabled them to render services . . . worthy of the best of veterans.

McClernand was next to Sherman, and the hardest fighting was in front of these two divisions. McClernand told me . . . that he profited much by having so able a commander supporting him.

A casualty to Sherman that would have taken him from the field . . . would have been a sad one for the troops engaged at Shiloh. And how near we came to this! . . . In addition to [taking two wounds], he had several horses shot during the day.

Late afternoon found the Confederates maintaining the offensive. According to newsman Albert Richardson, the Federal situation was gloomy:

On the right, Sherman still clung to [the bank of the creek], though farther back than in the morning; but the rest of the line. . . had swung around until its left rested on the river, two miles in the rear of its first position.

There were Union vessels on the river, including the gunboats Tyler *and* Lexington, *whose gunners were scanning the wooded battle zone for targets. Facing the Confederate advance on land, a last-ditch line of artillery had been set up by Colonel Joseph D. Webster, of Grant's staff.*

Says Jesse Young, the boy with Sherman's troops:

The woods were so full of smoke that scarcely anything could be seen. . . . Grant and Sherman [were] seemingly everywhere at the same moment, staying the retreat and reforming the lines and directing the artillery fire; and beyond, the yelling, crowding troops of Beauregard, making a final struggle to drive the Union men into the Tennessee. . . . All at once a booming sound came from the river. It was the. . . *Tyler* and the *Lexington.* . . .

Adds newsman Richardson:

Our infantry, also, made vigorous resistance; and Webster, riding along behind the artillery, shouted encouragingly: "Stand firm, boys; they can never carry this line. . . ."

The boys did stand firm, and though neither the land nor gunboat cannons did much damage, the worn-out rebels hesitated. This was extremely significant, and the chief [General

Grant], hitherto unmoved, showed his satisfaction with a sigh of relief and a faint smile.

Then he went over to the cheerful Sherman, to whom he said: "We will hold on for the rest of the day, and Buell will be up very soon."

Both agreed that the enemy had expended his fury. . . .

As Buell's men, crossing the river on transports, began to climb the bank and join Grant's battered lines, cheer after cheer went up. Their appearance, says Wills de Hass, "was a spectacle the most inspiriting that despairing men ever looked upon."

Jesse Young exults:

. . . spurning the mass of cowards that lined the banks, they went on the double-quick out to the front and into position, just in time to aid in checking the last advance of the Confederate army for the day.

Included with the reinforcements was a brigade of Kentuckians who had known and disliked Sherman at Muldraugh's Hill. Seeing him now with a bloodstained bandage on his hand, with his face blackened by powder smoke, and with the brim of his stovepipe hat torn by a shell fragment, they put their own hats on the tip of their bayonets and cheered him enthusiastically. Though Sherman made no response, he was deeply affected. This was about the first real approval he had had from the ranks since the war began.

Gradually the firing ceased [relates Wills de Haas]. The Sabbath closed upon a scene which had no parallel on the Western Continent. The sun went down in a red halo, as if the very heavens blushed and prepared to weep at the enormity of man's violence. Night fell upon, and spread its funereal pall over, a field of blood where death held unrestrained carnival!

Soon after dark the rain descended in torrents, and all through the dreary hours of that dismal night it rained unceasingly. The groans of the dying, and the solemn thunder of the gunboats [as they threw shells into the Confederate bivouacs] came swelling at intervals high above the peltings of the pitiless storm.

The rain extinguished several creeping brush fires started by the day's fighting, thus saving the lives of some of the helpless and unattended wounded. Other wounded men found the rain a blessing in that it helped to quench their terrible thirst.

Most of the Union soldiers and their officers, including Grant and Sherman, themselves lay in the rain that night, for Beauregard's men had their tents. Within these tents, and around great bonfires outside in the rain, the Confederates feasted on Yankee food and got drunk on Yankee whiskey. Others roamed the camps in search of additional plunder. These men considered themselves victorious, but their run of good fortune was actually over. By morning nearly 25,000 fresh Federals were on the field. And even many of the skulkers were now ready to fight.

"Monday morning at six o'clock," says Wills de Haas,

... the combined forces of Grant and Buell moved against the enemy. General Buell's fresh troops, with the division of Lew Wallace [from Crump's Landing], not engaged on Sunday ... pressed the enemy at all points. Steadily the army of the Union regained our camps....

Grant explains that the fighting lasted "until probably five o'clock in the afternoon, when it became evident the enemy was retreating."

My force was too much fatigued ... to pursue.... Night closed in cloudy and with a heavy rain, making the roads impracticable for artillery by the next morning. General Sherman, however, followed the enemy, finding that the main part of the army had retreated in good order. Hospitals with the enemy's wounded were found all along the road as far as pursuit was made. Dead bodies of the enemy and many graves were also found.

After a brief skirmish with the enemy's rear guard, Sherman returned to the camps at Shiloh. The dead and wounded were everywhere. Surgeons were busy amputating shattered limbs, the discarded parts forming ghastly red heaps. Other maimed men would have to lie with little care until civilian help arrived by steamboat from the North. The dead were buried hastily, with the Confederate victims being laid in trenches, sometimes stacked a half dozen deep. As for the hundreds of dead horses, attempts were made to burn them.

Sherman wrote to Ellen that the sights he saw "would have cured anybody of war." At the same time, he wrote their son Willie that "the Rebels ... are not afraid, and we must have more battles." He sent

*Willie and his brother Tommy a box filled with missiles he picked up on
the battlefield. "Some of them have powder in them, and you must keep
them away from the fire. Else they might burst and kill somebody."*

*Shiloh's final casualty figures staggered both the North and the
South. In killed, wounded, captured, and missing, the Federals lost over
13,000 men, while the Confederates lost about 10,700.*

*General Grant was criticized for not having had his troops in a better
state of preparation when the Confederates struck. The fault was that he
had misjudged his foe, but a rumor spread that he was drunk at the
crucial hour. Sherman defended him stoutly, saying many years later:
"Grant did drink, but never when anything important was pending."*

*At the war's beginning, Grant had been among those Northerners
who believed that the South might be beaten quickly. The spirit the
Confederates showed at Shiloh, after their defeats to the northward,
made him change his mind. He now agreed with Sherman that the war
would be a long one.*

*In his official report of the battle, sent to General Halleck's headquar-
ters in Saint Louis, Grant said:*

I feel it a duty . . . to a gallant and able officer, Brigadier-Gen.
W. T. Sherman, to make special mention. He not only was with
his command during the entire two days of the action, but
displayed great judgment and skill in the management of his
men. Although severely wounded in the hand on the first day,
his place was never vacant.

*General Halleck, who was senior in command to both Grant and Buell,
soon arrived at Pittsburg Landing and took charge of their combined
forces. The general reported to Washington:*

It is the unanimous opinion here that Brigadier-General W.
T. Sherman saved the fortunes of the 6th, and contributed
largely to the glorious victory on the 7th. . . . I respectfully request that he be made a Major-General of Volunteers, to date
from the 6th instant.

*Praise for Sherman came from other than just military sources. News-
papers that had been critical of him before Shiloh now recognized him as
a true champion of the cause. A Boston editor went further. After
reading one of Sherman's public defenses of Grant, he enthused: "How
his wrath swells and grows. He writes as well as he fights!"*

Cump's wife, his foster father, his brother John and others close to him, elated over his rise from the depths of depression to public acclaim, sent him their earnest congratulations. He was exceedingly gratified. His reputation, his pride, and his self-confidence were restored.

When his new commission arrived from Washington, Cump wrote Ellen that he wasn't sure he deserved it but added that "its possession completes the chain from cadet up, and will remain among the family archives when you and I repose in eternity."

~IV.

The Vicksburg Campaign

~ *T*he *Confederate army under General Beauregard had re-turned to Corinth, Mississippi, twenty miles southwest of Pittsburg Landing. Three weeks after the Battle of Shiloh, General Halleck, with an army reinforced to about 120,000 men, started for Corinth.*

But he moved slowly—virtually yard by yard—and he had the troops dig in deeply at every step. If Grant had been careless about security, Halleck was decidedly overcautious. It took him a month to reach Corinth, with the men feeling as though they had dug up the entire twenty miles of countryside. Arriving at the end of May, 1862, Halleck found that Beauregard had retreated southward. Halleck dug in at Corinth.

Grant had been placed in an awkward position. Halleck called him his "second in command," but gave him nothing to do. Grant wasn't one of Halleck's favorites. Sherman, on the other hand, had made the march from Pittsburg Landing in a position of honor; his division made up the extreme right of the army's right wing.

About this time [says De Bow Randolph Keim, a war corre-spondent who joined the army at Corinth], during a visit of Sherman to Halleck's headquarters, the latter casually referred to the intended departure the next morning of General Grant on thirty days' leave, alleging that to him the cause was not known. Sherman readily surmised it.

Hastening to General Grant's camp on the Monterey road, he

was surprised to find him located in an obscure wood, occupying, with his staff, five small tents, with camp chests and equipage piled around, and Grant himself in the midst, seated on a camp stool, assorting letters.

"General," said Sherman, having dismounted, "is it true you are going away?"

"Yes," replied Grant, going on with his assorting.

"And may I ask the reason?" . . .

"Sherman, you know. You know that I am in the way here. I have stood it as long as I can. . . ."

"Where are you going?"

"To St. Louis."

"Have you any business there?"

"Not a bit."

[Sherman] begged him in most earnest terms not to quit, illustrating his case by his own, adding: "Before the Battle of Shiloh, I was cast down by a mere newspaper assertion of being crazy. That single battle gave me new life, and now I am in high feather."

Grant was silent for some moments, but, consciously impressed, at length gave utterance to his resolve: "Sherman, I promise to wait, or not to go without seeing you again."

. . . Grant formally accepted his advice in a letter of June 6, to which Sherman on the same day from his camp made this characteristic response: "I am rejoiced at your conclusion to remain, for you could not be quiet at home for a week when armies were moving. . . ."

A month later, Halleck was called to Washington to become general in chief of all Federal armies, and Grant became commander at Corinth. But Halleck had diminished these forces, sending contingents to other strategic points in the western theater, and Grant was restricted in his plans for offensive operations.

The Union cause as a whole was no longer prospering. In the East the amphibious operation against Richmond had been turned back, and General Robert E. Lee was planning to take the offensive. In the middle zone—in eastern and central Tennessee—the Confederates were beginning to strike at the Union's positions. Only in Grant's department, which embraced western Tennessee and the northern border of Mississippi, was the Federal front fairly stable.

This department had become a very important one. The Union's great objective in the West was to gain control of the full length of the

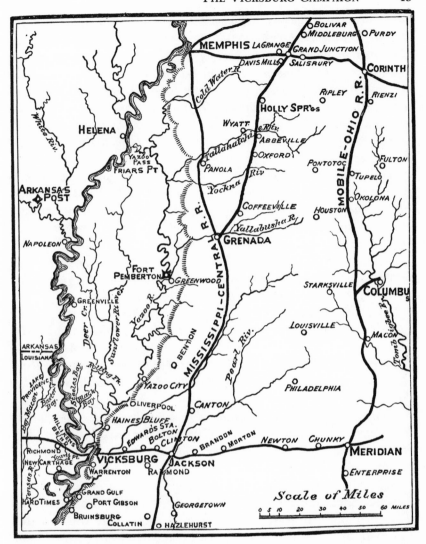

THE VICKSBURG CAMPAIGN.

Mississippi River, which would cut the Confederacy in two, denying the Eastern states the cattle, grain, and other supplies they needed from the West. At the same time, the Union would gain a convenient highway for further operations.

On April 28 New Orleans, at the mouth of the river, had fallen to a Federal fleet operating from the Gulf of Mexico, and on June 6 a fleet in the river's northern waters had taken Memphis, Tennessee, in Grant's department. Memphis and New Orleans were some 400 miles apart. Lying about halfway between them, on a set of bluffs on the east bank, was the heavily fortified town of Vicksburg, Mississippi, the key to complete control of the river.

While Union war planners both on the field and in Washington were looking toward Vicksburg, Sherman became military administrator of the newly captured Memphis, operating from a camp nearby. He was sensitive to the welfare of the Confederate citizens, even setting up a program of aid for the poor. But soon he began to realize that the people he was treating so fairly were secretly helping Confederates who were bearing arms.

While maintaining the system he had established, Sherman began to exact stern retribution for specific acts against the Union. When guerrillas in the town of Randolph, north of Memphis, fired on an unarmed Union steamboat bearing civilian passengers, he ordered the town burned, except for a single house "to mark the place."

When slaves who had run away from their masters became numerous in Memphis, Sherman put them to work for the Union. In return they received food, clothing, and a pound of tobacco a month.

Early that autumn came the news from Washington that President Lincoln had issued the preliminary draft of his Emancipation Proclamation. All slaves in states hostile to the Union were to be freed on January 1, 1863. Sherman did not approve. "Are we to feed all the Negroes?" he asked. "Freedom don't clothe them, feed them, and shelter them."

While at Memphis, Sherman developed his theory of "collective responsibility" in regard to the war. To his brother John he wrote, "It is about time the North understood the truth, that the entire South, man, woman, and child, is against us. . . ."

He expanded the thought in a report to Grant at Corinth:

We cannot change the hearts of the people of the South, but we can make war so terrible that they will realize the fact that however brave and gallant and devoted to their country, still they . . . should exhaust all peaceful remedies before they fly to war.

In a letter to his daughter Minnie, then attending school at Notre Dame, Indiana, Sherman explained:

I have been forced to turn families out of their houses and homes and force them to go to a strange land because of their hostility, and I have today been compelled to order soldiers to lay hands on women to force them to leave their homes to join their husbands in hostile camps.

Think of this, and how cruel men become in war when even your papa has to do such acts. Pray every night that the war may end.

Hundreds of children like youself are daily taught to curse my name, and every night thousands kneel in prayer and beseech the Almighty to consign me to perdition.

In another letter to Minnie, Sherman said that it troubled him to be a general in the Union service, since he had to be harsh with people he knew and liked, among them close associates of his years in the South. "Every day I meet old friends who would shoot me dead if I were to go outside of camp and who look on me as a brutal wretch."

Among the Federals, esteem for Sherman had increased steadily since Shiloh. Though he demanded much of his troops, he was equally hard on himself. When rations ran short, he shared the shortage. And when it was necessary for his men to endure bad weather he often endured it with them. Though he was apt to swear roundly at incompetence, he was usually thoughtful when dealing with his staff. One officer wrote, "He . . . has cheering amiability. The men love him."

Toward the end of autumn, Ellen came to Memphis to visit with Cump, bringing Tommy with her. Less than a year earlier, Tommy had heard his father called crazy on a street in Lancaster; here the boy saw him treated with profound respect. Tommy spent much of his time with the soldiers, even taking his blanket and sleeping with them. Ellen found Cump in bright spirits, though he was very thin. She wrote her father, "He looks more wrinkled than most men of sixty." Cump was not yet 43.

In early December, Sherman met with Grant at Oxford, Mississippi, southeast of Memphis, where plans were made for a move against Vicksburg. It was to be a cooperative affair. While Grant led an expedition southward through Mississippi toward Vicksburg's rear, Sherman was to take an amphibious force down the river and assault the defenses on the town's northern flank.

Admiral David Dixon Porter, son of Commodore David Porter, hero of the War of 1812, was the naval commander working with Sherman. Their great flotilla, made up of gunboats, transports, and other vessels, got under way from Memphis on December 20. The trip downriver went well, though frequent stops had to be made to gather firewood for the steam boilers.

The 30,000 troops, soon tiring of standing along the rails and watching the shore, turned to card games and conversation in thick

DAVID D. PORTER.

UNION GUNS at Chickasaw Bayou. From a wartime sketch.

groups. The blue smoke of tobacco drifted everywhere, and those men who chewed were pleased to have the broad river as a spittoon.

Unknown to Sherman and Porter, Grant's part in the operation came to nothing. Some of the Confederates got around behind him and cut his supply lines; he was forced to turn back. This doomed Sherman's attack to failure. According to Porter:

We reached Chickasaw Bayou in safety, but the army did not get much farther.... No one, at that time, had any idea of the magnitude of the defenses that had been erected in every quarter to keep a foe out of Vicksburg....

Operating from low, swampy ground, Sherman assaulted Chickasaw Bluffs, just north of Vicksburg, on December 29. He was soon repulsed. An alternate operation begun the next day had to be cancelled when a dense fog settled over the swamps.

Again in Porter's words:

To add to Sherman's difficulties, the rain came on—and such a rain! The heavens seemed trying to drown our army; the naval vessels and transports were the only arks of safety. The level lands were inundated, and there were three feet of water in the swamps where our army was operating....

[On January 1, 1863] our disheartened troops returned to the transports.... It was still raining, and the current ran so strong in the river that the vessels had to be fastened securely to the trees. The wind howled like a legion of devils....

That night General Sherman came on board my flagship, drenched to the skin. He looked as if he had been grappling with the mud and got the worst of it. He sat down and remained silent for some minutes....

I said at length, "What is the matter?"

"I have lost seventeen hundred men, and those infernal reporters will publish all over the country their ridiculous stories about Sherman being whipped, etc."

"Only seventeen hundred men!" I said. "Pshaw! That is nothing; simply an episode in the war. You'll lose seventeen thousand before the war is over.... We'll have Vicksburg yet before we die. —Steward, bring some punch for the general and myself."

"That's good sense, Porter!" exclaimed the general, "and I am glad to see you are not disheartened. But what shall we do now? I must take my boys somewhere and wipe this out."

I informed the general that I was ready to go anywhere. "'Then," said he, "let's go and thrash out Arkansas Post."

This was a fort on the Arkansas River that had been bypassed on the trip down the Mississippi. Also called Fort Hindman, it mounted eleven heavy guns and held a garrison of about 5,000 men. Porter goes on:

We started as soon as possible and arrived at the Post.... I attacked it with three ironclads and several smaller vessels, and in three hours disabled all the guns. General Sherman surrounded the place with his troops, and, after heavy losses [on the Federal side], it surrendered—the fort, in charge of naval officers, to me, and the Confederate army ... to General Sherman.

After partially destroying the fort and sending the prisoners northward, the Federals made their way back down the Mississippi to Milliken's Bend, about twenty-five miles upriver from Vicksburg. Late in January, General Grant arrived to take command of renewed efforts against the Confederate stronghold.

Vicksburg bristled with heavy guns along its river front, discouraging all Federal thoughts of a direct assault, and its northern flank was protected by a great area of wet bottom land, a part of which Sherman had encountered a month earlier.

The Federals failed not only in their attempts to get through the northern swamps but also to bypass the town through similar bottom land across the river, on the Louisiana, or western, shore. The Louisiana efforts involved the laborious digging of canals for Porter's vessels, the idea being to get the vessels and the troops safely around Vicksburg's guns and into a position where the town might be approached from the south. One by one, the various ventures had to be abandoned.

In cooperation with Admiral Porter, Grant at length devised a plan aimed at breaking the long and frustrating deadlock. The army was to pick its way through the swamps on the western side of the river to a point well below the town, with Sherman's corps staying behind temporarily to confuse the enemy. Porter was to take a part of the fleet directly past Vicksburg's batteries in the night. Once the army and the navy were reunited down the river, the army would be ferried across for a campaign around Vicksburg's rear. Large quantities of supplies had to be carried along, since Grant would be cutting himself off for a time from all connection with his northern depots.

According to Colonel William F. Vilas, of a regiment from Wiscon-

PASSAGE of the Vicksburg batteries by Admiral Porter's fleet. Sherman is aboard small boat in foreground, his role that of a spectator. He is about to pay a visit to Porter's flagship.

sin, the plan was so daring as to be considered unmilitary by many of Grant's subordinates:

It is an interesting commentary upon its military nature that his warmest friend and ablest general, Sherman, instantly endeavored to dissuade him, both by personal interview and written communication, representing how grossly he was overriding the fundamental axiom of strategy in exposure of his army, and begging that at least he would invoke the opinions of his generals in a council of war.

Others of his best officers took similar ground. Grant, however, never resorted to a council of war, and remained unshaken. . . .

On the night of the 16th of April, Admiral Porter ran the batteries. . . . It was a wild night. The Confederates were ready, and previously-prepared buildings and other bonfires, both in Vicksburg and on the Louisiana point opposite, illuminated the river soon after the start.

The fleet was for over two hours under fire, and every vessel was repeatedly struck, the gunboats returning the fire vigorously. Yet all passed the ordeal, no gunboat being disabled; and only one steamboat lost. This having been set on fire was abandoned by the crew.... Yet strange to say, though some were wounded, not a life was lost.

General Sherman, out in the river in a small boat watching the awful scene, himself picked up from the water the pilot of the lost steamer. [Actually, this was done by the crew of a second small boat in Sherman's charge.]

Adds Admiral Porter, who led the procession of vessels in his flagship, the Benton:

I had just passed the last battery... when I was hailed by someone in a boat, *"Benton* ahoy!"

"Halloo!" I replied, and presently I recognized the voice of General Sherman.

"Are you all right, old fellow?"

"Come on board and see," I replied, and Sherman came over the side to hear about our fortunes.

"One man's leg cut off by a round shot; half a dozen shell and musket ball wounds," I said.

"... There are a lot of my boys on the point ready to help you if you want anything.... Good night! I must go and find out how the other fellows fared."

... He would have liked to have been in the storm of shot could he have done so with propriety.

Porter's successful passage of the batteries did not increase Sherman's faith in Grant's overall plan. Back at his headquarters farther up the river that same night, Sherman wrote Ellen: "I tremble for the result. I look upon the whole thing as one of the most hazardous and desperate moves of this or any other war."

Sherman remained above Vicksburg as the rest of the army began joining the navy a dozen miles below. Grant's next problem was to get his troops across the river. There was danger that Confederate General John C. Pemberton, top commander in the Vicksburg area, would bring a strong force to oppose the crossing.

Relates Colonel Vilas:

On the 27th of April ... Grant wrote Sherman of his desire to have a seeming attack on Haynes' Bluff [north of Vicksburg, a few miles from Chickasaw Bayou] to distract the enemy's attention from his operations. Yet it looked hard to ask Sherman to undergo again an apparent repulse, who had been so sorely abused in Northern newspapers and derided in the South for his failure there in the Christmas season before. And so Grant's letter to him ran:

"The effect of a heavy demonstration in that direction would be good so far as the enemy are concerned, but I am loth to order it, because it would be so hard to make our own troops understand that only a demonstration was intended, and our people at home would characterize it as a repulse. I therefore leave it to you whether to make such a demonstration. . . ."

Sherman's reply the next day was characteristic: "I will take ten steamers and ten regiments and go up the Yazoo as close to Haynes' as possible without putting the transports under the rifled guns of the enemy. We will make as strong a demonstration as possible.

"The troops will understand the purpose, and will not be hurt by the repulse. The people of the country must find out the truth as they best can; it is none of their business. You are engaged in a hazardous enterprise, and, for good reasons, wish to divert attention. That is sufficient for me, and it shall be done. . . ."

Grant explains:

My object was to compel Pemberton to keep as much force about Vicksburg as I could until I could secure a good footing on high land east of the river. [Sherman's] move was eminently successful, and, as we afterwards learned, created great confusion about Vicksburg, and doubts about our real design.

The crossing was made. at Bruinsburg, some thirty miles below Vicksburg. Advance units quickly pushed inland a few miles to Port Gibson, where on May 1 they defeated a Confederate detachment that came to meet them.

There now remained [says Colonel Vilas] . . . the quick concentration of the scattered army. Sherman was already coming with speed; other divisions in rear were pushed forward. . . . The supreme moment had arrived. Grant had at hand, counting Sherman's, about 33,000 men, unembarrassed by baggage or useless trains, stripped to fight, as hardy, confident, ardent, as ever went to battle.

Instead of concentrating at once upon Vicksburg, Grant turned his attention in the direction of Jackson, about forty miles due east of the objective, where a new Confederate force was gathering. After defeating a 5,000-man detachment near the town of Raymond, he marched upon Jackson. The 12,000 men assembled there were easily dispersed, and Grant was now prepared to head for Vicksburg. But first he set Sherman to destroying Jackson as a railroad center and as a manufacturer of Confederate supplies. Grant relates:

Sherman and I went together into a manufactory which had not ceased work on account of the battle, nor for the entrance of Yankee troops. Our presence did not seem to attract the attention of either the manager or the operatives, most of whom were girls.

We looked on for a while to see the tent cloth which they were making roll out of the looms with "C. S. A." woven in each bolt. There was an immense amount of cotton, in bales, stacked outside.

Finally I told Sherman I thought they had done work enough. The operatives were told they could leave and take with them what cloth they could carry. In a few minutes, cotton and factory were in a blaze.

Grant headed west toward Vicksburg without Sherman, who remained at Jackson to pursue the job of destruction. But there wasn't sufficient time to finish, for Grant, finding a strong force under General Pemberton in his path, sent word back to Sherman to hurry forward.

On this march Sherman once rode up to a well to get a drink and, seeing a book on the ground, asked a soldier to hand it up to him. It was entitled The Constitution of the United States, *and the name Jefferson Davis was penned on the title page. To his surprise, Sherman learned that he was on the plantation owned by the President of the Confederacy, now absent.*

Before Sherman joined Grant, the Battle of Champion's Hill had been fought (May 16). This was another victory for the Federals and caused the Confederates to fall back to the Big Black River, about ten miles east of Vicksburg. Sherman helped to push the Confederates across the river, after which they fled to Vicksburg, securing themselves behind about eight miles of defenses that semicircled the town's rear, from river bank to river bank. During the pursuit, Sherman was in the lead, heading for the right of the defenses, north of town.

On the 18th [says Grant] I moved along the Vicksburg road

in advance of the troops and as soon as possible joined Sherman. My first anxiety was to secure a base of supplies on the Yazoo River above Vicksburg. Sherman's line of march led him to the very point . . . occupied by the enemy the December before when he was repulsed.

Sherman was equally anxious with myself. Our impatience led us to move in advance of the column and well up with the advanced skirmishers. . . . The bullets of the enemy whistled by thick and fast for a short time. In a few minutes Sherman had the pleasure of looking down from the spot coveted so much by him the December before. . . .

Adds Colonel Vilas:

Generously and enthusiastically he there told Grant that to that minute he had felt no assurance of success, never could see the end clearly before; but now had ended one of the greatest campaigns of history, whatever the final result.

There is a picture for some painter's brush! Those friends, chief heroes of the war, outlined on the sky above that hilltop. . . .

Grant soon invested the long semicircle of Confederate defenses with a longer semicircle of his own, Sherman remaining on the right. Word was sent to Admiral Porter to use his gunboats to menace Vicksburg from the front. Grant first tried to take the rear defenses by assault but was twice repulsed with many casualties. He then resorted to a siege.

Both the defenses and the town were bombarded. Many of the civilians took refuge in caves dug in the town's hillsides. As Grant undertook the digging of a great trench system in front of the defenses, his sharpshooters plied their skill, with the Confederates replying. Heavier firing often developed, with artillery joining in.

Sherman's front [says Charles A. Dana, a civilian observer from Washington] was at a greater distance from the enemy than that of any other corps, and the approaches less advantageous, but he began his siege works with great energy and admirable skill. Everything I saw of Sherman . . . increased my admiration for him. He was a brilliant man and an excellent commander of a corps.

The siege continued for six weeks. As summed up by Colonel Vilas:

Naturally, the Confederate authorities [in the East] strove to raise an army for relief. But Halleck [in Washington] ... sent Grant the abundant reinforcements he instantly saw were needful. And Grant, failing in no care, fortified his rear until he was almost within a second Vicksburg. . . .

So of course there was fighting, mining [i.e., the digging of tunnels under the Confederate fortifications in an attempt to breach them with explosives] and countermining; day and night were active and noisy, and many a heroic deed was done along the seven or eight miles of investment. Enough there was for a long and charming tale by a competent pen.

And Vicksburg fell, spectacularly on the nation's birthday, with 31,600 prisoners, and 172 cannon, 60,000 small arms and much ammunition; "the largest capture of men and material ever made in war" up to that time.

So soon as known, Port Hudson's commander gave up that fortress, a necessary sequence. [Port Hudson was a smaller post about 150 miles farther down the river.]

And the Mississippi ran unvexed to the sea. The Confederacy was hopelessly split in twain. The backbone of the rebellion was broken. . . . The enemy was confined to their eastern states, and the assistance they had so much benefited by from west of the Mississippi was forever lost.

The great victory gave Sherman his "first gleam of daylight in this war." He believed now that the Confederacy must fall.

One day during the siege Grant had heard Sherman say to a group of civilian officials who had come down from the North: "Grant is entitled to every bit of the credit for this campaign. I opposed it. I wrote him a letter about it."

But for this speech [Grant explains] it is not likely that Sherman's opposition would have ever been heard of. His untiring energy and great efficiency during the campaign entitle him to a full share of all the credit due for its success. He could not have done more if the plan had been his own.

V.

Toward a New Command

*D*uring the same days of July, 1863, that saw the war in the West reach a climax at Vicksburg, the Union forces in the East won a decisive victory at Gettysburg, Pennsylvania. The preceding ten months had seen the Eastern men lose three out of four great battles to General Lee, but Gettysburg redeemed their failures.

The people of the South were staggered by the twin defeats, but they were far from ready to quit. They had small hope of recouping their military fortunes, but figured that if they maintained a stiff resistance the North might yet grow sick of the bloodshed and agree to grant them independence to end it.

Immediately after Vicksburg's surrender, Grant ordered Sherman and his divisions eastward toward Jackson, whose war facilities they had partially destroyed seven weeks earlier. The town had become the base of operations for the Confederate relief army, commanded by General Joseph Johnston, formerly of the Eastern theater. Sherman not only drove Johnston away but finished the job of destruction. He tried to protect private property, worrying in particular about art objects, but the men got out of hand, setting fires in unauthorized places. Jackson soon became "Chimneyville."

Sherman told the anguished citizens that the blame lay not with his men and himself but with the leaders of secession. The way to stop such outrages, he said, was to stop the war. Sherman was now convinced that the quickest way to victory was to lay waste to Southern property. In the *end, he believed, such a policy would prove a blessing to both the North and the South.*

On July 22 Sherman ordered his divisions back to their camps east of Vicksburg for a rest period. "I have the handsomest camp I ever saw," he wrote to Ellen in Ohio, and she came south for a visit, bringing the four oldest children. Sherman was happy. He had just become a brigadier general in the regular army (his major generalship of volunteers was only a temporary commission), which meant that his financial future was on a good footing; he would need no more help from his foster father to keep his family comfortable.

Cump was particularly pleased with his son Willie, now nine years old. The boy showed a lively interest in the army's affairs. During reviews and drills he liked to sit behind his father on his horse. Captain C. C. Smith, a friend to Sherman and commander of the Thirteenth Battalion of United States regulars, made Willie an honorary sergeant. The boy was provided a uniform, and he learned the manual of arms.

One of Sherman's men, Private Edward Chase, was to say later that the troops were daily favored with the sight

... of the bright little face of "Sergeant" Willie. The little fellow ... won all hearts by his winning ways and his fondness for playing soldier. At every part of the camp he was a welcome visitor, and many a father petted him as a relief from the terrible feeling of loneliness.

While the troops about Vicksburg lay idle in the heat of late summer, the war entered a new phase, with the middle zone (central and eastern Tennessee) coming to prominence. At the beginning of the year the Union's Army of the Cumberland, under General William S. Rosecrans, had bested General Braxton Bragg's Army of Tennessee at Murfreesboro, opening the way for an advance southeastward to Chattanooga, on Tennessee's southern border. An important railroad center, the town was known as The Gateway to the Deep South.

Mid-September found the Union troops just south of Chattanooga, along Chickamauga Creek, where they encountered their old foes and were badly defeated. Retreating northward into the town, they took up a position with their backs to the Tennessee River, the Confederates ringing them on the south and east. In grave danger, the Federals sent out calls for reinforcements.

Grant ordered Sherman to take the greater part of his corps toward the trouble zone by way of Memphis, which meant a boat trip up the Mississippi. Sherman's wife and children joined him on his steamer. He

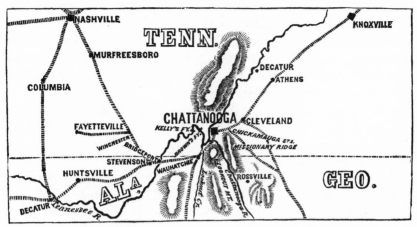

CHATTANOOGA and vicinity.

planned to send them on up the river when he debarked at Memphis.

Even as the trip started, Willie fell sick, and it was learned that he had typhoid fever. Critically ill by the time he was carried to the Gayoso House, a Memphis hotel, the boy soon died. While his stricken parents tried to comfort each other, Willie's friends of the Thirteenth arranged a military funeral. On October 4 the small casket, draped with a flag, was conveyed to a steamer for its trip northward in Ellen's care.

Late that night, alone in his room at the Gayoso House, Sherman wrote a letter to Captain Smith of the Thirteenth:

My Dear Friend: I cannot sleep tonight till I record an expression of the deep feelings of my heart to you and to the officers and soldiers of the battalion for their kind behavior to my poor child. . . .

The child that bore my name, and in whose future I reposed with more confidence than I did in my own plan of life, now floats a mere corpse, seeking a grave . . . with a weeping mother, brother, and sisters clustered about him.

For myself I ask no sympathy. On, on I must go, to meet a soldier's fate or live to see our country rise superior to all factions, till its flag is adored and respected by ourselves and by all the powers of the earth.

But Willie was, or thought he was, a sergeant in the Thirteenth. I have seen his eyes brighten, his heart beat, as he beheld the battalion under arms and asked me if they were not *real* soldiers. . . . God only knows why he should die thus young. . . .

Please convey to the battalion my heartfelt thanks, and assure each and all that if, in after years, they call on me or mine and mention that they were of the Thirteenth Regulars when Willie was a sergeant, they will have a key to the affections of my family that will open all it has; that we will share with them our last blanket, our last crust.

Your friend,

W. T. Sherman, *Major General.*

Early the next morning, Cump wrote Ellen:

Sleeping, waking, everywhere I see poor little Willie. His face and form are as deeply imprinted on my memory as were deep-seated the hopes I had for his future. . . . I will go on to the end, but feel the chief stay to my faltering heart is gone. . . . I will try and make poor Willie's memory the cure for the defects which have sullied my character . . . all that is captious, eccentric and wrong.

Sherman was more resilient than he supposed. A few days later he was able to lose himself in his part of the campaign to relieve the Union troops at Chattanooga, about 300 miles to the east. On November 13, six weeks after Willie died, Sherman reached Bridgeport, some twenty miles west of his destination, having tarried along the way to make repairs to the Memphis & Charleston Railroad, used by the Federals as a supply line. By this time Grant was in Chattanooga and had assumed command of the endangered forces. One of the generals with him was Oliver O. Howard, who says of the date November 14:

In the evening several officers were sitting together in an upper room, when General Sherman, having left his marching column back at Bridgeport, arrived upon the scene. He came bounding in, after his usual buoyant manner. General Grant, whose bearing toward Sherman differed from that with other officers, being free, affectionate, and good humored, greeted him most cordially.

Immediately after the "How are you, Sherman?" and the reply, "Thank you, as well as can be expected," he extended to him the ever welcome cigar. This Sherman proceeded to light, but without stopping his ready flow of hearty words, and not even pausing to sit down.

Grant arrested his attention by some apt remark, and then said: "Take the chair of honor, Sherman," indicating a rocker with a high back.

"The chair of honor? Oh, no! That belongs to you, general."

Grant, not a whit abashed by this compliment, said: "I don't forget, Sherman, to give proper respect to age."

"Well, then, if you put it on that ground, I must accept."

That night I had the opportunity of hearing the proposed campaign discussed as never before. Sherman spoke quickly but evinced much previous knowledge and thought. Grant said that Sherman was accustomed on horseback to "bone" his campaigns, i.e., study them hard from morning till night. . . .

After the general plan of battle had been canvassed and settled upon, Sherman returned to his troops at Bridgeport and marched them to us.

The three-day Battle of Chattanooga (November 23, 24, and 25) resulted in another great victory for Grant. With Sherman on the left, General George Thomas in the center, and General Joseph Hooker on the right, Grant swept Braxton Bragg's Confederates from their heights south and east of the town (from Lookout Mountain and Missionary Ridge), putting them into full retreat. Bragg stopped only when he got to Dalton, Georgia, some twenty miles to the southeast. Chattanooga, the all-important Gateway to the Deep South, was now firmly in Union hands. Grant became the North's "man of the hour."

Immediately after Chattanooga, Sherman was dispatched on a march of over 100 miles northeastward to Knoxville, where a Confederate force was besieging General Ambrose Burnside and his command. Made under winter conditions, the march was a hard one, but nothing more than skirmishing was required to break the siege, the Confederates retiring as the relief force approached. Sherman soon returned to Chattanooga.

To a Southern woman who complained to Sherman that his men had done a lot of stealing on the Knoxville expedition, the general replied, "Madam, my soldiers have to subsist themselves even if the whole country must be ruined. . . . War is cruelty. . . . The crueler it is, the sooner it will be over."

Grant had moved his headquarters to Nashville, 135 miles northwest of Chattanooga, and Sherman went there to see him on December 21. Generals Gordon Granger and Grenville Dodge were with Grant at the time, and the four commanders, all shabbily dressed, went unrecognized by soldiers and civilians alike as they spent the afternoon enjoying a tour of the town.

According to war correspondent De Bow Keim:

In order to while away the evening, Sherman suggested the

theater. They paid their way in . . . and sat down in the front balcony row. *Hamlet* was the bill. The place was crowded with soldiers.

Unable to stand such foul murder of his favorite hero, Sherman exclaimed excitedly: "Dodge, that is no way to play Hamlet!"

"General, don't talk so loud; some of the boys will discover us, and then there'll be a scene not in the play."

But his indignation was hard to repress.

In the grave scene, during the soliloquy over the skull of Yorick, a soldier jumped up yelling from a back seat: "Say, pard, was it Yank or Reb?"

The house came down.

Grant, making for the exit, observed in sotto voce: "Sherman, we had better get out of here or we'll be in a worse scrape than the enemy can set up for us."

Out they went, in hasty retreat, just as the boys caught on.

From Nashville, Sherman went home to Lancaster Ohio, for Christmas. Willie was still much on his mind. Ellen and the other children were living at the Ewing mansion, with Ellen having undertaken the care of her elderly parents, who were ailing. Thomas Ewing was still basically sound, but Maria was in her last illness. Both were very proud of their foster son, thankful they had lived long enough to see him rise to fame.

Wherever Cump went he was treated as a hero, with the crowds including reporters, photographers, and autograph-seekers. The attention was gratifying only to a point. Cump was driven to making some gruff responses and some quick departures from the scene.

Sherman left home as the year 1864 began, going down the Mississippi to Vicksburg. Muzzling the press to ensure secrecy, he led an expedition eastward through Mississippi to Meridian, a Confederate railroad center and supply base. His route was marked by destruction, with much of the town itself being burned.

Returning to Vicksburg, Sherman reported, "We bring in some 500 prisoners, a good many refugees, and about ten miles of Negroes." The blacks had followed the army to the freedom granted them by Lincoln's Emancipation Proclamation. Exulting in their camps with hand-clapping, singing, dancing, and praying, they regarded Sherman as their savior.

At the beginning of March, Sherman, with a small party, descended the Mississippi River to New Orleans to consult with General Nathaniel

BLACKS celebrating their freedom.

Banks, who was planning an expedition west of the river and had asked to borrow 10,000 of Sherman's men. The arrangements made, Sherman steamed back up the river, his destination Memphis. On the way he received momentous news: General Grant had gone to Washington to assume command of all the armies of the United States.

Grant came west briefly to consult with Sherman, the meeting taking place at Nashville on March 17. It was Grant's plan to take personal command of the Army of the Potomac, then in northern Virginia. This was the army that had been fighting General Lee for the past two years in an attempt to capture Richmond. Sherman was given the job in the West that Grant's promotion had left vacant, that of commander of the Military Division of the Mississippi.

In the words of one of Sherman's generals, Jacob D. Cox:

His courage and activity had been abundantly proven, but his capacity for the independent command of a large army was to be tested. His nervous and restless temperament, with a tendency to irritability, might have raised a doubt whether he would be successful . . . but experience showed that he had the rare faculty of becoming more equable under great responsibilities and in scenes of great excitement.

At such times his eccentricities disappeared, his grasp of the situation was firm and clear, his judgment was cool and based upon sound military theory as well as upon quick practical judgment, and no momentary complication or unexpected event could move him from the purposes he had based on full previous study of contingencies.

His mind seemed never so clear, his confidence never so strong, his spirit never so inspiring, and his temper never so amiable as in the crisis of some fierce struggle. . . .

The South had two major armies, the one under Lee that was protecting Richmond, and the one lying at Dalton, Georgia, recovering from its defeat at Chattanooga and now commanded by Joseph Johnston.

As soon as possible, Grant wanted to strike at both armies at the same time, he himself pressing southward to Richmond, and Sherman starting at Chattanooga and advancing southward through Dalton to Atlanta, a total distance of about 120 miles.

Sherman rode the train eastward with Grant as far as Cincinnati. According to S. M. Bowman, the colonel in Sherman's army who became a student of his career:

During the journey, they had a full and free conference as to the plan of operations in the approaching campaign, and a complete understanding of the work to be done by each. In the parlor of the Burnet House at Cincinnati, bending over their maps, the two generals, who had so long been inseparable, planned together . . . the great campaigns of Richmond and Atlanta . . . and, grasping one another firmly by the hand, separated, one to the east, the other to the west, each to strike at the same instant his half of the ponderous deathblow.

~VI.

South to Atlanta

~S *herman had only about six weeks to prepare his campaign. The gathering of his supplies depended upon a single line of rails from Louisville, Kentucky, nearly 300 miles north of Chattanooga. This line had been bringing vitally needed rations to Tennessee's civilians, many of whom were friendly to the Union, and a roar of anguish went up when Sherman announced that all trains must now carry nothing but military supplies.*

Explains David P. Conyngham, one of the newspaper correspondents who retained enough favor with Sherman to be allowed to join his expedition:

He believed the safety and support of his army paramount to all other considerations. He had a long campaign before him, a long and uncertain line of communications to guard from a vigilant enemy.

"Let the citizens go south, or to the rear. . . . The campaign must open with thirty days' surplus rations at Chattanooga."

This was Sherman's logic. And good logic it was for the safety of the army, but fatal, in their terrible starving condition, to the unfortunate sufferers of East Tennessee. A hegira of poor, forlorn refugees then commenced, followed by human suffering that might appall the angels.

Eliminating civilian rations from the trains was only a partial solution

to Sherman's needs at Chattanooga. According to F. Y. Hedley, adjutant of an Illinois regiment, "supplies failed to accumulate."

Cutting red tape with a stroke of his pen, Sherman ordered all railroad cars reaching Louisville, from whatever direction, to be loaded with supplies and sent to the front; and in spite of the angry protests of railroad officials all over the country, his order was obeyed to the letter.

This solved the supply problem, but there were many other things to be done. Sherman had to oversee the preparations of his cavalry and

REFUGEES in East Tennessee.

*artillery units, his surgeons and their assistants, his telegraphers and
signalmen, his pioneers, his civilian workmen.*

*In the end, says Adjutant Hedley, all departments of the army were
well organized:*

It was this complete system of organization . . . that raised this
army to so high a degree of efficiency and gave to its chief such
a wonderful mastery over it. Well might he say . . . "The least
part of a general's work is to fight a battle."

Napoleon once remarked that he had overrun Europe with
the bivouac [i.e., with his encampments providing only the

barest necessities, this for the sake of mobility]. Sherman had caught the same inspiration. Wagon trains were cut down to the smallest possible number of wheels and animals. . . .

Each man carried his gun and accoutrements, 40 rounds of ammunition in his cartridge-box and 160 more in his pockets, knapsack, or haversack. His blanket and light rubber blanket were made into a long roll, the ends tied together, so as to admit of being carried upon the shoulder. This roll generally contained an extra shirt, a pair of socks, and a half-section of a "dog tent," . . . which, when buttoned to the half carried by a comrade, made a very fair shelter for two men. . . .

The provision issued to the soldier was a much abridged ration, but it brought up the total weight of his burden to a good 30 pounds or more, no light load to carry for days at a time, in all weather, and over all kinds of roads. He habitually had a three-days' supply of hard bread and fat pork, and this was to last from seven to ten days in case of necessity.

But if Uncle Sam limited the boys as to their bread and meat, he more than made it good with his lavish issues of sugar and coffee. . . .

The troops were now ready to move out of Chattanooga. "The pomp and circumstance of glorious war" were to be left behind. . . . The army was at its fighting weight, stripped to the buff, ready and willing to give and take hard knocks.

Sherman had more than 100,000 men to go against Johnston's 65,000. Johnston, however, had the advantage of being on the defensive; he could choose his own battlefields. Moreover, he was in friendly country and his supply lines were short.

During the final days of preparation, Sherman and Grant kept in close touch with each other. Again in Hedley's words:

They used the telegraph freely . . . exchanging views with reference to the movements of the armies, East and West . . . each conforming his course to that of the other. In short, complete confidence and concert of action existed. . . .

May 4, 1864, General Grant crossed the Rapidan, moving toward Richmond; and twelve hours later General Sherman put his army in motion in the direction of Atlanta. . . .

The march was begun amid the glories of spring. According to C. E. Benton, a soldier from New York, "the woods were fragrant with flow-

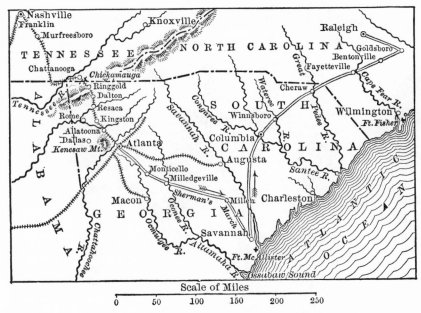

MAP SHOWING ROUTES of Sherman's last three campaigns: From Chattanooga to Atlanta, from Atlanta to Savannah, and from Savannah to Raleigh.

ers." But the old Chickamauga battlefield, with its somber sights, was directly in the army's path. Benton continues:

Soon we came to trees cut down by shell; nearly all of the trees were marked and torn by bullets and shells. Mounds of earth, with the middle sunken in, showed where dozens of men had received scant burial. Here and there a foot protruded; or a hand with the skin dried to the bones was seen extended from a grave as if beckoning to us. Further on we came to numbers of bodies which had not been buried. Then we passed Chickamauga Creek.... Continuing southeast, we confronted the enemy....

Now began several weeks of minor fighting and deft maneuvering, over plains and mountains, under hot sun and drenching clouds, through choking dust and clinging mud. The guns, though not working at their maximum, were rarely silent for long at a time.

Adjutant Hedley says that Sherman's strategy was "marvelous,"
... and he found a worthy adversary in General Joseph E. Johnston.... Move succeeded move, like rook and pawn on the

SHERMAN in Georgia.

chessboard, one giving a check here, the other there. Sherman maneuvered so as to gain position after position with the minimum loss of men and material; Johnston retreated so skillfully before him [in the direction of Atlanta] that he scarcely lost a tin cup.

Entrenching and fortifying became an art on both sides. Explains Union War correspondent De Bow Keim:

As soon as a command got into position, if the enemy were near, the work began. In a single night the position was secured against reasonable odds. To this extent every fighting command was its own pioneer corps. General Sherman improved on this system by organizing in each division a pioneer corps of Negroes seeking refuge within his lines, whom he fed and paid $10 a month.

The scheme acted to a charm. The Negroes, backed by the incentive of hallelujahs and freedom, grub and greenbacks, made good use of the night and slept as chance offered during the day, while the worn and tired soldier took his rest as he could at night, and was ready, fresh, and fierce for the fray during the day.

Sherman himself, with work to do both night and day, slept only in snatches. And even during these periods he often rested poorly, being troubled by asthma, a longstanding condition not helped by his cigar smoking and presently aggravated by the heightened tension.

General Oliver Howard says that one morning early in the campaign

... Sherman, who had worked all night, was sitting on a log with his back against a tree, fast asleep. Some men marching by saw him, and one fellow ended a slurring remark by: "A pretty way we are commanded!"

Sherman, awakened by the noise, heard the last words. "Stop, my man!" he cried. "While you were sleeping last night, I was planning for you, sir. And now I was taking a nap."

Many of the people of the farms and towns in Sherman's path fled as he approached, and the abandoned properties were looted and ravaged, not only by straggling soldiers and camp followers but by blacks who suddenly found themselves free. Some of the families who remained in their homes went relatively unmolested, while others were driven away. Flames and towering smoke were a common sight.

"To realize what war is," Sherman wrote Ellen, "one should follow our tracks."

Sherman's general route was along the railroad that led from Chattanooga to Atlanta, which he used as his supply line. Sections torn up by the Confederates, as well as the bridges they burned, were quickly replaced. At length, says Adjutant Hedley:

... the enemy was fully convinced that Sherman and his men were all but omnipotent, and that destructive measures were of little avail to arrest their progress. Indeed, there was a story ... to the effect that Johnston had determined to blow up an important railroad tunnel in order to stop the invaders, whereupon one of his men remarked, "There isn't no use in that. ... Sherman carries along duplicates of all the tunnels."

During this stage of the campaign, which advanced Sherman about three quarters of the way to Atlanta, the stiffest fighting occurred at Resaca (May 14–15) and at New Hope Church (May 25–28). A dozen miles from New Hope Church was Kennesaw Mountain, where Sherman launched a major attack against Johnston on June 27. The Union troops were repulsed with sharp losses. New maneuvers on Sherman's part, however, obliged Johnston to continue his withdrawal toward Atlanta, and he took up a strong position just north of the town on July 10.

THE BATTLE OF RESACA. Union skirmish
line nears base of mountain as
Confederate artillery fires from top.
Smoke on left of sketch is that of Union
artillery.

During these last maneuvers, Sherman took time out from his host of responsibilities to answer a letter he received from Mrs. Annie Gilman Bower, a woman he had known as a young girl during his early days in the South and who now lived in Baltimore. The letter was published widely in both Northern and Southern newspapers:

Your welcome letter of June 18th came to me amid the sound of battle; and, as you say, little did I dream when I knew you . . . that I should control a vast army pointing, like a swarm of Alaric, towards the plains of the South. . . .

If I know my own heart, it beats as warmly as ever toward those kind and generous families that greeted us with such warm hospitality in days long past. . . . And yet they call me barbarian, vandal, and a monster, and all the epithets that language can invent that are significant of malignity and hate.

All I pretend to say: On earth, as in heaven, man must submit

to an arbiter. He must not throw off his allegiance to his Government or his God without just reason and cause. The South had no cause. . . . Had we declined battle, America would have sunk . . . meriting the contempt of all mankind. . . .

I would not subjugate the South in the sense so offensively assumed, but I would make every citizen of the land obey the command, submit to the same that we do—no more, no less. . . .

Even yet my heart bleeds when I see the carnage of battle, the desolation of homes, the bitter anguish of families; but the very moment the men of the South say that instead of appealing to war they should have appealed to reason, to our Congress, to our courts, to religion, and to the experience of history—then will I say peace, peace. . . .

I hope when the clouds of anger and passion are dispersed, and truth emerges bright and clear, you and all who knew me

JOHN B. HOOD.

in early years will not blush that we were once close friends. . . .

For failing to stop Sherman, General Johnston now lost his command, by order of President Davis, to General John B. Hood. Possessing none of Johnston's shrewdness, Hood was known as an aggressive fighter, even after the war had cost him a leg and the use of an arm.

Sherman's campaign for Atlanta had been in progress for a little over two months. Meanwhile, some 500 miles to the northeast, General Grant had fought a series of bloody battles on his way to Richmond. He was now besieging the Confederate capital and its southern neighbor, Petersburg, from the east, but the defenses of the two cities remained firmly in Lee's hands. With the siege threatening to become a long one, Grant hoped that Sherman would soon brighten the general war picture by taking Atlanta.

General Hood managed to hold the town for six weeks, during which time its environs were the scene of almost continual skirmishing and fighting. Sherman brought the town itself under shellfire, and at night the explosions were accompanied by awesome colorations on the ground and in the sky.

Hood, living up to his reputation as a fighter, initiated three battles at points about the town: the battles of Peach Tree Creek (July 20), Atlanta (July 22), and Ezra Church (July 28). The Confederates were repulsed all three times. Sherman at length moved to cut off Hood's railroad communications running southward from Atlanta, and this resulted in the Battle of Jonesboro (August 31), which Sherman won.

Hood now had no choice but to evacuate Atlanta, which he did during the night of September 1. Fireworks rocked the town as he blew up ammunition reserves that could not be carried away. Some of the town's well-to-do civilians decided to leave with the army. Union correspondent David Conyngham learned a little later that

The delicate drawing-room miss that could never venture half a mile on foot, with her venerable parents now marched out, joining the solemn procession.

Confusion and disorder prevailed in every place.... Shrieking, hissing shells rushed into the air, as if a thousand guns were firing off together. We plainly heard the noise at Jonesboro.

How terrifying must it be to the trembling, affrighted fugitives, who rushed to and fro, and believed, with every report, that the Yankees were upon them....

Hood and those civilians who accompanied him got away safely, thanks to a delaying action fought by General William J. Hardee. Sherman was more interested in seizing his prize than in pursuing, and the fighting soon came to an end.

Since the first shots had been fired north of Dalton in early May, each side had taken upwards of 30,000 casualties—killed, wounded, captured, and missing.

The fall of Atlanta, says correspondent Conyngham, was "the crowning point of Sherman's great campaign."

Hood had been outgeneralled, outmanoeuvred, and out-flanked, and was now trying to concentrate his scattered army.... Next morning Sherman resolved to retire to the defenses of Atlanta, there to give his wearied army time to recuperate after its unparalleled campaign of four months' marching and fighting....

In a military point of view, Atlanta was of vital importance.... It was the key to the network of railroads extending to all portions of the Gulf States, and on the inception of the war was at once selected as a government depot and manufacturing center; so rolling mills, foundries, machine shops, laboratories, and shops for the manufacture of all kinds of government articles were established here....

The city had suffered much from our projectiles. Several

A CONFEDERATE CAVE, or "bombproof," in Atlanta. House shows shellfire damage.

houses had been burned, and several fallen down. In some places the streets were blocked up with the rubbish.... Few houses escaped without being perforated....

One woman pointed out to me where a shell dashed through her house as she was sitting down to dinner. It upset the table and things, passed through the house, and killed her neighbor in the next house....

Almost every garden and yard around the city had its cave. These were sunk down with a winding entrance... so that pieces of shell could not go in.... Some of these caves, or bombproofs, were fifteen feet deep and well covered.... In some cases it happened that our shells burst so as to close up the mouths of the caves, thus burying the inmates in a living tomb.

The same correspondent reports that Sherman's personal entry into the town was made "without parade or ostentation," that he merely rode straight toward the house chosen as his headquarters.

The citizens looked out from their doors and windows, eager to catch a glance of the man whose name had now become so famous.... Officers mounted on prancing steeds looked far more consequential than the great conqueror himself, and cast their eyes from window to balcony to see if any fair eyes were admiring their gracious selves. The fair eyes had fled, and those remaining would fain wither them....

Sherman had already telegraphed Washington: "Atlanta is ours, and fairly won."

For President Lincoln, the news was most opportune. He was running for a second term, with his conduct of the war the leading issue, and his chances had seemed dim, the pace of victory having slowed after Gettysburg, Vicksburg, and Chattanooga. Now he had another spectacular triumph to his credit. He said in his congratulatory message to Sherman:

The marches, battles, sieges, and other military operations that have signalized the campaign must render it famous in the annals of war, and have entitled those who have participated therein to the applause and thanks of the nation.

General Grant telegraphed Sherman from his siege lines at Richmond and Petersburg:

I have just received your dispatch announcing the capture of Atlanta. In honor of your great victory, I have ordered a salute to be fired, with *shotted* guns, from every battery bearing upon the enemy. The salute will be fired within an hour, amid great rejoicing.

Adjutant Hedley says that Sherman ordered both messages read to the various units of the army:

And now that the troops ... learned with what joy the news was received at home, they gave way to a protracted jubilee. The brass and martial bands, which had been silent all the long way from Chattanooga to Atlanta, now played their most exultant airs; and the men vied with the instruments in making noise expressive of great joy.

All were happy and smiling, from the commander-in-chief to the humblest private in the ranks, and even the bray of the half-starved government mule seemed mellow and melodious as it added to the din.

~VII.

The March to
the Sea

    While deliberating the question of his next move in the theater of war, Sherman set about consolidating his hold upon Atlanta. Explains war correspondent De Bow Keim:

His first proposition was the removal of the entire civil population from within its limits, with orders to go north or south, as they should elect. . . .

As early as September 4 [1864] he gave notice of his purpose to General Halleck [serving in Washington as Grant's chief of staff], concluding: "If the people raise a howl against my barbarity and cruelty, I will answer that war is war and not popularity seeking. If they want peace, they and their relatives must stop the war."

Sherman's evacuation order aroused all the furor he anticipated, with even General John Hood joining the angry chorus. To an appeal to reconsider that he received from the town's mayor and two councilmen, Sherman replied:

I . . . give full credit to your statements of the distress that will be occasioned, and yet shall not revoke my orders, because they were not designed to meet the humanities of the case but to prepare for the future struggles in which millions of good people outside of Atlanta have a deep interest. . . .

    . . . I assert that our military plans make it necessary for the inhabitants to go away, and I can only renew my offer of services to make their exodus in any direction as easy and comfortable as possible.

You cannot qualify war in harsher terms than I will. War is cruelty, and you cannot refine it. And those who brought war into our country deserve all the curses and maledictions a people can pour out. I know I had no hand in making this war, and I know I will make more sacrifices today than any of you to secure peace. But you cannot have peace and a division of our country. . . .

You might as well appeal against the thunderstorm as against these terrible hardships of war. They are inevitable, and the only way the people of Atlanta can hope once more to live in peace and quiet at home is to stop the war. . . .

We don't want your Negroes or your horses or your houses or your lands, or anything you have. But we do want, and will have, a just obedience to the laws of the United States . . . and if it involves the destruction of your improvements, we cannot help it. . . .

. . . the South began the war by seizing forts, arsenals, mints, custom-houses, etc., etc. . . . I myself have seen . . . hundreds and thousands of women and children fleeing from your armies and desperadoes, hungry and with bleeding feet. . . .

Now that war comes home to you, you feel very different. You deprecate its horrors; but did not feel them when you sent carloads of soldiers and ammunition, and moulded shells and shot, to carry war into [Unionist areas of] Kentucky and Tennessee, to desolate the homes of hundreds and thousands of good people who only asked to live in peace at their old homes and under the government of their inheritance.

But these comparisons are idle. I want peace, and believe it can only be reached through union and war. . . . But, my dear sirs, when peace does come, you may call on me for anything. Then will I share with you the last cracker, and watch with you to shield your homes and families against danger from every quarter.

Now you must go, and take with you the old and feeble, feed and nurse them, and build for them in more quiet places proper habitations to shield them against the weather until the mad passions of men cool down and allow the Union and peace once more to settle over your old homes at Atlanta.

Many of the citizens came to Sherman with special problems related to their departure. One man said later that most of the appellants found the general "patient, gentlemanly, and obliging—as much so as he could be . . . consistently with his prescribed policy."

[A] lady with whom I conversed . . . represents him as being very kind and conciliatory in his deportment towards her and others who visited him. He expressed much regret at the necessity which compelled him to order the citizens of Atlanta from their homes; but stated in justification of his course . . . that it was impossible for him to subsist his army, and feed the citizens too, by a single line of railroad; and that . . . he thought it was humanity to send them out of the city, where they could obtain necessary supplies.

He took the little child of my friend in his arms and patted her rosy cheeks, calling her a "poor little exile" and saying he was sorry to drive her away from her comfortable home, but that war was a cruel and inexorable thing, and its necessities compelled him to do many things which he heartily regretted.

By this time Sherman was exchanging views on his next move with General Grant, whose own situation remained virtually unchanged, with Lee's lines before Richmond and Petersburg showing no signs of cracking. Grant sent one of his letters to Sherman by the hand of an aide, Colonel Horace Porter, who came down the railroad from Chattanooga during the third week in September. Porter relates:

Upon reaching Atlanta, I went at once to General Sherman's headquarters. My mind was naturally wrought up to a high pitch of curiosity to see the famous soldier of the West, whom I had never met. He had taken up his quarters in a comfortable brick house . . . opposite the Courthouse Square.

As I approached I saw the captor of Atlanta on the porch, sitting tilted back in a large armchair, reading a newspaper. His coat was unbuttoned, his black felt hat slouched over his brow, and on his feet were a pair of slippers very much down at the heels. . . . He was just forty-four years of age. . . . With his . . . tall, gaunt form, restless hazel eyes, aquiline nose, bronzed face, and crisp beard, he looked the picture of "grim-visaged war."

My coming had been announced to him by telegraph, and he was expecting my arrival at this time. I approached him, introduced myself, and handed him General Grant's letter. He tilted forward in his chair, crumpled the newspaper in his left hand while with his right he shook hands cordially, then pushed a chair forward and invited me to sit down. His reception was exceedingly cordial, and his manner exhibited all the personal peculiarities which General Grant, in speaking of him, had so often described.

After reading General Grant's letter, he entered at once upon an animated discussion of the military situation East and West, and as he waxed more intense in his manner the nervous energy of his nature soon began to manifest itself.

He twice rose from his chair and sat down again, twisted the newspaper into every conceivable shape, and from time to time drew first one foot and then the other out of its slipper, and followed up the movement by shoving out his leg so that the foot could recapture the slipper and thrust itself into it again.

He exhibited a strong individuality in every movement, and there was a peculiar energy of manner in uttering the crisp words and epigrammatic phrases which fell from his lips as rapidly as shots from a machine-gun.

I soon realized that he was one of the most dramatic and picturesque characters of the war.

Porter remained in Atlanta for two or three days, during which Sherman used him as a sounding board for a bold idea he was beginning to form—that of taking his army on an expedition of destruction from Atlanta to the sea, temporarily abandoning all communications with the North, subsisting on the land and its people. Such a march, he reasoned, would not only divest the South of vital resources but would spread discouragement in epidemic proportions.

When Porter left, he carried a letter from Sherman to Grant that closed with these words: "I admire your dogged perseverance and pluck more than ever. If you can whip Lee, and I can march to the Atlantic, I think Uncle Abe will give us twenty days' leave of absence to see the young folks."

Sherman was not yet ready to give up his railroad communications northward to Chattanooga, and in October he was obliged to march from Atlanta to put an end to raids on the line by General Hood, who had revitalized his army. Hood did some serious damage near Allatoona and at several other places, then retreated westward into Alabama. Sherman followed across the border, then desisted.

Hood was expected next to invade Tennessee in an attempt to draw Sherman northward, but Sherman had no intention of becoming a party

CONFEDERATE ARTILLERY firing on distant Union troops at Allatoona.

to this game. Leaving a substantial force under General George Thomas to defend Tennessee against Hood, Sherman returned to Atlanta.

Both Lincoln and Grant were dubious about Sherman's proposed march to the sea, but he won their permission to proceed with his plans. Sherman himself was confident, informing Grant by telegraph, "I can make this march, and make Georgia howl!"

Says Adjutant Hedley:

Events during the last week in October and the first ten days in November, 1864, were stirring enough. The railroad ... was repaired.... Every train going north was loaded to its utmost capacity with the wounded and infirm, with surplus artillery, and, in fact, almost everything that the men could not carry on their backs. Returning trains brought only the most needed articles—hard bread, pork, coffee, sugar, and ammunition. It was evident even to those in the ranks that some important, if not desperate, undertaking was at hand. . . .

Hedley goes on to explain that the troops guarding the railroad at last destroyed most of its length, then joined the army at Atlanta:

There was now not a Federal soldier between Atlanta and Chattanooga, and the hills and plains which had lately echoed the fearful din of artillery and musketry, and had been alive with masses of fiercely contending human beings, were . . . still and desolate. . . . But . . . here, there, and everywhere were graves of those who wore the blue and those who wore the gray, each surmounted by a board upon which were rudely cut, by knives of comrades, the name, company, and regiment of him who lay beneath.. . .

On the night of November 15th, the torch was applied to the railroad shops, foundries, and every one of the many buildings that had been used in fitting out the armies of the enemy in this vast "workshop of the Confederacy," as Atlanta was called.

That night Major George Ward Nichols, an aide-de-camp to Sherman, wrote in his diary:

A grand and awful spectacle is presented to the beholder in this beautiful city, now in flames. . . . The heaven is one expanse of lurid fire; the air is filled with flying, burning cinders; buildings covering two hundred acres are in ruins or in flames; every instant there is the sharp detonation or the smothered booming sound of exploding shells and powder concealed in the buildings, and then the sparks and flames shoot away up into the black and red roof, scattering cinders far and wide.

Attempts were made to protect private property, but many homes were soon afire. Again in Adjutant Hedley's words:

The Twentieth Corps, which had garrisoned Atlanta while the remainder of the army was pursuing Hood . . . were the last to leave the city, and as they marched out, the fine silver band of the 33rd Massachusetts . . . played "John Brown." The men took up the words wedded to the music, and high above the roaring flames, above the crash of falling walls, above the fierce

SHERMAN leaving Atlanta. Column of smoke rises from the ruins.

crackling of thousands of small-arm cartridges in the burning buildings, rose the triumphant refrain, "His truth is marching on!"

Sherman's long columns marched from the environs of Atlanta the next morning. Many of the men turned for a last look at the ruined city, which was still smoldering under a great pall of smoke. The weather was sunny, blue, and crisp; and in spite of the uncertainties ahead the men were exhilarated. Again, a band struck up the "John Brown" march, and Sherman said later that he never heard the chorus of "Glory, glory, hallelujah!" sung with more spirit.

During an interlude of relative quiet, one of the marchers called out to Sherman as he rode by, "Uncle Billy, I guess Grant is waiting for us at Richmond!"

Sherman's goal at this time was not Richmond, but Savannah, Georgia, about 500 miles south of the coveted Virginia city.

As the marchers sang, joked, and laughed, Sherman was struck by the extent of his responsibilities. "Success would be accepted as a matter of course, whereas, should we fail, this march would be adjudged the wild

adventure of a crazy fool." On the bright side, Sherman expected little
resistance from the enemy, and he had complete confidence in his army.
  Adjutant Hedley calls the army "a remarkable body of men."

Sixty thousand in round numbers, it was an army of veterans
who had served an apprenticeship of more than three years at
their profession.... This army of veterans was also an army of
boys. The old men... had been very generally worn out and
sent home or to the hospital.

It was the "little devils" (as Sherman once called them in...
[my] hearing...) who remained and could always be depended
upon to carry their load, march all day, and be ready for a frolic
when they went into bivouac at night. Very many of them,
notwithstanding three years of soldiering, were not old enough
to vote.... But... what they did not know about campaigning
was not worth inquiring into.

Each soldier was practically a picked man.... He was fertile
of resources, and his self-confidence was unbounded.... His
confidence in... "the old man" (General Sherman) was such
that he did not disturb himself on that score. He was heading
south[east] instead of north, and this was ample assurance that
Thomas was taking care of Hood, and that Grant was "holding
Lee down."

... This army, which had been marching light from Chattanooga to Atlanta, was now simply reduced to what it had on,
and that was not much.... No army ever marched with less
impedimenta, and none adapted itself so completely or cheer-
fully to its conditions.

The army marched in four columns, the various corps pursuing parallel roads. These columns were sometimes five, sometimes fifteen miles apart. Their combined front was from forty
to sixty miles.... The skirmishers and flankers of each corps
spread out until they met those of the corps next to them on
either side....

In front of each corps marched a regiment of cavalry or
mounted infantry. Frequently these troops, with the aid of the
infantry brigade at the head of the column, were able to brush
aside the enemy [units of Georgia militiamen and detachments
of General Joseph Wheeler's cavalry] without much trouble,
and without halting the main column....

This was a section of country which the war had not disturbed until this moment. It was literally a land overflowing

A PARTY of Sherman's foragers on a Georgia plantation.

with milk and honey, and well was it for the army that such was
the case [for rations soon became a problem]. . . .

The emergency produced the forager, commonly known as
"the bummer." . . . Sherman . . . specified his duties; but cer-
tainly no one could have been more surprised than the general
himself to see the aptitude of this creature for his task, and the
originality of his methods. . . .

When the bummer left the column . . . he either went on
foot . . . or bareback on some broken-down horse or mule. . . .
At the first farmhouse he came to, he looked about for a fresh
mount. If it was to be had, he helped himself; if not . . . nine
times out of ten some darkey belonging to the place would pilot
him to where the stock was hidden in the woods or swamps.

Then he would search the place for provisions, and soon
have his animal, and perhaps two or three others, loaded down

with poultry, meats, meal, sweet potatoes, honey, sorghum, and frequently a jug of applejack; or he would find a wagon and load it. . . .

But he worked hard for what he obtained. In many cases, smoke-houses and barns were empty, and when he had nearly abandoned all hope of finding anything, some old darkey . . . would direct him to search under the house. Often a hint from the same source would lead him to open what appeared to be a newly-made grave, but which proved to be the repository of the provisions he had been vainly seeking.

In few instances were the inhabitants found at home. The majority, terrified by the horrible stories published by their newspapers of the rapine and rapacity of the dreaded "vandal Yankees," had fled, taking with them what they could. When the premises were abandoned, the bummer made a clean sweep, appropriating everything he wanted, and a great many things he did not want.

If the Negroes on the place told stories of great cruelty they had suffered, or of bitter hostility to the Union, or if there were bloodhounds about which had been used to run down slaves, the injury was generally avenged by the torch.

When the bummer found women and children, he was usually as courteous as circumstances admitted. He would pass the time of day with the old lady, inquire when she had heard from "the old man," and whether he was with [Hood] or Lee, winding up with kissing the baby.

Behind this excess of good nature, it must be confessed, lay, in part, a selfish motive. The bummer . . . learned all that was to be known of the neighbors farther down the road, whom he expected to raid the next day.

Almost as important to Sherman as his bummers were the men he assigned to destroying Georgia's railroads. Many miles of track were taken up, the ties burned, and the sections of rail heated and bent around trees to form what became known as "Sherman's neckties."

Everywhere that Sherman rode he attracted crowds of blacks who greeted him as a kind of messiah. He says that they "shouted and prayed in their peculiar style, which had a natural eloquence that would have moved a stone." Some heeded the general's advice that they stay where they were, at least for the present; but thousands of others, with their belongings and their plundered goods on their backs, in carts, and in wagons drawn by horses or mules, followed in the army's wake.

BLACK REFUGEES in wake of Sherman's army.

According to a Confederate cavalry officer, J. P. Austin, who observed Sherman's progress:

When the crowd became too burdensome, the Federals would take up their bridges at the crossing of some river and leave their poor, deluded followers on the opposite bank to ponder over the mutability of human plans and to cast a longing look at the receding forms of their supposed deliverers.

Union war correspondent David Conyngham says that the greater part of Sherman's army saw "little or no fighting," and that for many of the men the march developed into "one delightful picnic." As the looting intensified, Conyngham saw:

Men with pockets plethoric with silver and gold coins; soldiers sinking under the weight of plate and fine bedding materials; lean mules and horses with the richest trappings of Brussels carpets and hangings of fine chenille; Negro wenches, particularly good-looking ones, decked in satin and silks, and sporting diamond ornaments; officers with sparkling rings that would set Tiffany in raptures. . . .

Conyngham goes on to explain that destruction of property became rampant, with more and more fires being set:

This is the way Sherman's army lived on the country. They were not ordered to do so, but I am afraid they were not brought to task for it much either.

The marching distance from Atlanta to Savannah was nearly 300 miles. Along the way was Milledgeville, then Georgia's capital. The governor and the legislature fled, "without waiting," as one soldier put it, "to present Sherman with the key to the city."

Here a mock legislature was set up, with the soldiers voting, after a spirited debate, to repeal Georgia's ordinance of secession and restore the state to the Union. Afterward, under the influence of captured liquor, the "legislators" proceeded to vandalize the capitol building, failing to spare even the state library. The books that were not stolen were thrown out windows into the mud, where they were trampled by passing horses and men.

With Sherman having abandoned all contact with the North, there was much worried speculation as to what was happening to him. Says General Grant:

The Southern papers in commenting upon Sherman's movements pictured him as in the most deplorable condition: stating that his men were starving, that they were demoralized and wandering about almost without object, aiming only to reach the seacoast and get under the protection of our navy. These papers got to the North and had more or less effect upon the minds of the people, causing much distress to all loyal persons—particularly to those who had husbands, sons or brothers with Sherman.

Mr. Lincoln seeing these accounts, had a letter written asking me if I could give him anything that he could say to the loyal people that would comfort them. I told him there was not the slightest occasion for alarm; that with 60,000 such men as Sherman had with him, such a commanding officer as he was could not be cut off. . . . He might possibly be prevented from reaching the point he had started out to reach, but he would get through somewhere . . . and even if worst came to worst he could return North.

I heard afterwards of Mr. Lincoln's saying to those who would inquire of him about the safety of Sherman's army that Sherman was all right: "Grant says they are safe with such a general, and that if they cannot get out where they want to, they can crawl back by the hole they went in at."

Sherman's march had its gentler moments. According to an unnamed correspondent:

Sitting before his tent in the glow of a campfire one evening, General Sherman let his cigar go out to listen to an air that a distant band was playing. The musicians ceased at last. The general turned to one of his officers: "Send an orderly to ask that band to play that tune again."

A little while, and the band received the word. The tune was "The Blue Juniata," with exquisite variations. The band played it again, even more beautifully than before. Again it ceased; and then, off to the right, nearly a quarter of a mile away, the voices of some soldiers took it up. . . .

The band, and still another band, played a low accompaniment. Camp after camp began singing. The music of "The Blue Juniata" became, for a few minutes, the oratorio of half an army.

Leaving behind him a swath of desolation sixty miles wide, Sherman reached the environs of Savannah on December 10, three and a half weeks after leaving Atlanta. He placed Savannah under siege, at the same time moving against a waterfront installation, Fort McAllister. The fort was captured on December 13, enabling Sherman to establish contact with a Federal fleet in nearby waters. One of the vessels held a mountain of mail from home, which gave rise to general rejoicing.

At this time there was rejoicing in the North as well. The first people who heard the news by telegraph, the dwellers in the cities, rushed out into the streets shouting, "Sherman has reached Savannah!" The words flew from the cities to the towns, hamlets, and farms. People danced and sang, and church bells pealed. After nearly three and a half years of war, the foundations of the Confederacy were finally crumbling.

Savannah soon capitulated, its inadequate garrison—about 10,000 men—slipping away in the night. In a message to President Lincoln dated December 22, Sherman said:

I beg to present you as a Christmas gift the city of Savannah, with one hundred and fifty heavy guns and plenty of ammunition; also about twenty-five thousand bales of cotton.

Lincoln replied with a letter that began, "Many, many thanks for your Christmas present. . . ."

Sherman himself got a Christmas present in the form of news from

Tennessee. On December 15 and 16, Thomas and Hood had fought a great battle at Nashville, and Hood's army was decimated. Sherman had been counting on Thomas: "His brilliant victory . . . was necessary to mine at Savannah to make a complete whole. . . ."

With Grant still stalled before Richmond and Petersburg, Sherman's stock soared. Congress talked of making him at least Grant's equal in the army's command structure, and perhaps even his superior. This did nothing but rouse Sherman's ire: "I will accept no commission that would tend to create a rivalry with Grant."

When an official from the North came to him in Savannah and tried to disparage Grant, Sherman said angrily:

"It won't do, sir; it won't do at all! Grant is a great general. He stood by me when I was crazy, and I stood by him when he was drunk. And now, by thunder, we stand by each other!"

Sherman was gentle with Savannah. Though he made the city a base of Union operations, he allowed its 20,000 people to remain in their homes. They were grateful, and he found that "good social relations at once arose between them and the army."

Adjutant Hedley says that the occupational period was "a continual round of merry-making."

If the few male inhabitants remaining were somewhat formal and distant, ample amend was made by the ladies, who were generally cordial; and each little knot of soldiers made acquaintance with fair ones, glad to entertain and be entertained with cards, dance, and song.

The city held large numbers of needy people, and Sherman gave them food from his stores. This bounty was augmented by sympathetic people in the North who, feeling that the war was nearly over, dispatched mercy vessels to Savannah.

A newspaper correspondent from Boston, Charles Carleton Coffin, discovered that Savannah's people "generally were ready to live once more in the Union."

The fire of Secession had died out. . . . At a meeting of the citizens, resolutions expressive of gratitude for the charity bestowed by Boston, New York, and Philadelphia were passed, also of a desire for future fellowship and amity. . . .

Society in the South, and especially in Savannah, had undergone a great change. The extremes of social life were very wide apart before the war. They were no nearer the night before Sherman marched into the city. But the morning after, there was a convulsion, an upheaval, a shaking up and a settling down of all the discordant elements. The tread of that army of the West, as it moved in solid column through the streets, was like a moral earthquake, overturning aristocratic pride, privilege, and power.

Old houses, with foundations laid deep and strong in the centuries, fortified by wealth, name, and influence, went down beneath the shock. The general disruption of the former relations of master and slave, and forced submission to the Union arms, produced a common level. . . .

On the night before Sherman entered the place, there were citizens who could enumerate their wealth by millions; at sunrise the next morning they were worth scarcely a dime. Their property had been in cotton, Negroes, houses, land, Confederate bonds and currency, railroad and bank stocks.

Government had seized their cotton; the Negroes had possession of their lands . . . [and] had become freemen; their houses were occupied by troops; Confederate bonds were waste paper; their railroads were destroyed, their banks insolvent. They had not only lost wealth, but they had lost their cause.

~VIII.

Northward
Through the Carolinas

~ *Clearly, Sherman had been right in his conviction that he could accomplish more by attacking the South's material resources then by concentrating upon her armies. His method of warfare seemed grossly cruel, but it saved lives on both sides. Sherman merely shrugged at the knowledge that future generations the world over, lacking a full understanding of his aims, were likely to regard him as a ruthless vandal. He found it curious that a general who destroyed property was invariably considered a greater brute than one who fought bloody battles.*

Sherman's triumph at Savannah was marred by a private tragedy. He learned that a baby son he had never seen had died of a pulmonary ailment. "I hoped he would be spared us," Cump wrote Ellen, "to fill the great void in our hearts left by Willie."

Cump believed that Willie would have understood the significance of the march from Atlanta. "Oh, that Willie were living," Cump said in the same letter. "How his eyes would brighten and his bosom swell with honest pride. . . ."

Though Sherman found deep satisfaction in having proved himself and his military theories, he wasn't overly impressed with his fame. He hadn't really sought this, regarding each new task as a weightier duty rather than as a steppingstone in a great career. When he learned during the Atlanta campaign that the North was beginning to view him as presidential timber, he disavowed all interest in the idea:

"If forced to choose between the penitentiary and the White House for four years . . . I would say the penitentiary, thank you."

*While the streets of Savannah rang with celebrations on New Year's
Eve, 1864, Sherman sat alone in his quarters writing his brother John
that he wished he could slip away from his responsibilities*

... and see more of my family, which is growing up almost
strangers to me. I have now lost Willie and the baby without
even seeing him, and were it not for General Grant's confidence in me, I should insist upon a little rest. As it is, I must go
on.

*In early January, 1865, Sherman received a letter from his old friend
General Halleck in Washington:*

While almost everyone is praising your great march ... there
is a certain class having now great influence with the President ... who are decidedly disposed to make a point against
you. I mean in regard to "Inevitable Sambo." They say that you
have manifested an almost *criminal* dislike of the Negro, and
that you are not willing to carry out the wishes of the Government in regard to him, but repulse him in contempt.

*The charges had only the weakest foundation in fact. It was true that
Sherman had resisted Washington's instructions that he recruit black
men as soldiers; he preferred to employ them as laborers and servants—
in which capacity he was glad to have them.*

*Sherman had come to accept the death of slavery as a proper outcome
of the war. "The South deserves all she has got for her injustice to the
Negro," he wrote Halleck. "But," he added, "that is no reason why we
should go to the other extreme."*

*It was Sherman's conviction that the former slave "must pass through
a probationary state before he is qualified for utter and complete freedom."*

*Halleck was told, "I do and will do the best I can for the Negroes, and
feel sure that the problem is solving itself slowly and naturally. It needs
nothing but our fostering care."*

*On January 11, Secretary of War Edwin M. Stanton arrived from
Washington on a revenue cutter to consult with Sherman. One of
Stanton's intentions was to investigate Sherman's attitude toward the
Negro, and he requested that a group of black leaders be summoned to a
special meeting. Part way through the meeting, Sherman was asked to
leave the room for a few minutes. He did so, though he considered the
request an affront to his position.*

EDWIN M. STANTON.

"What is the feeling of the colored people in regard to General Sherman?" Stanton asked. "Do they regard his sentiments and actions as friendly to their rights and interests—or otherwise?"

The answer was given by an ordained minister of the Baptist church, the Reverend Garrison Frazier:

We looked upon General Sherman, prior to his arrival, as a man in the Providence of God especially set apart to accomplish this work, and we unanimously feel inexpressible gratitude to him, looking upon him as a man that should be honored for the faithful performance of his duty.

Some of us called on him immediately upon his arrival, and it is probable that he would not meet the Secretary of War with more courtesy than he met us. His conduct and deportment toward us characterized him as a friend and gentleman.

We have confidence in General Sherman, and think that whatever concerns us could not be under better management.

It was now three weeks since Savannah's fall, and both civil and military affairs were running smoothly. Relates aide-de-camp George Nichols:

It seemed as if Sherman and his army had determined to

IN THE MARSHES of South Carolina.

become permanent residents of the city.... Yet... it was thoroughly understood by all the intelligent veterans who composed the legions of Sherman that so long as Lee and his forces stood defiant at the Rebel capital, Richmond was the real objective of our campaign.

How and when we were to reach that point [about 500 miles to the north] were the questions discussed throughout the camp; but our men said that while "Uncle Billy" had the matter in his hands, it was sure to go right....

The capture of Savannah was but a pivot upon which he swung his army; this campaign was but a part of the *grand idea.* The 15th of January saw the troops actually set in motion for the new campaign, and it was soon known that South Carolina was to be the next field of operations.

This northward march promptly met with a two-week delay caused by heavy winter rains that swelled the streams and swamps. During this period, Sherman spent one of his nights sleeping on the floor of an abandoned country mansion. Growing cold when his fireplace fire burned low, the general rose and renewed the flames with an old wooden mantel clock and the remains of a bedstead. He later referred to this as "the only act of vandalism that I recall done by myself personally during the war."

Sherman was to inflict even more damage upon South Carolina than he did upon Georgia. This was the state that had led the secessionist movement, and on its seacoast were Charleston Harbor and Fort Sumter, where the first shots had been fired against the Union flag.

Even the people of Georgia wanted to see South Carolina suffer. Many Georgians had told Sherman they would forgive him for what he had done to their state if he would be at least as hard on South Carolina.

Says Union war correspondent David Conyngham:

There can be no denial . . . that the feeling among the troops was one of extreme bitterness towards the people of the State of South Carolina. . . . Threatening words were heard from soldiers who prided themselves on "conservatism in house-burning" while in Georgia, and officers openly confessed their fears that the coming campaign would be a wicked one.

Just or unjust as this feeling was towards the country people of South Carolina, it was universal. I first saw its fruits at Rarysburg, where two or three piles of blackened brick and an acre or so of dying embers marked the sight of an old revolutionary town—and this before the column had fairly got its "hand in."

At McBride's plantation, where General Sherman had his headquarters, the out-offices, shanties, and surroundings were all set on fire before he left. I think the fire approaching the dwelling hastened his departure. . . .

If a house was empty, this was *prima facie* evidence that the owners were rebels [and not Union sympathizers], and all was sure to be consigned to the flames. If they remained at home, it was taken for granted that *everyone* in South Carolina was a rebel, and the chances were the place was consumed. . . .

The pine forests were fired, the resin factories were fired, the public buildings and private dwellings were fired. The middle of the finest day looked black and gloomy, for a dense smoke arose on all sides, clouding the very heavens. At night the tall pine trees seemed so many huge pillars of fire. . . .

Vandalism of this kind, though not encouraged, was seldom punished. . . .

Foragers and bummers heralded the advance of the army, eating up the country like so many locusts. These fellows, mounted on scraggy old mules or cast-off horses, spread themselves in one vast advance guard, and sometimes went twenty miles ahead of the main columns.... The bummers of different corps sometimes fought among one another about the spoils, and other times fraternized together in order to dislodge the troublesome enemy....

In every instance the Negroes ... proved our friends, giving us valuable information relative to the enemy's movements; also acting as scouts and spies, informing us where the enemy had concealed their cattle, and the like. The poor, despised Negroes looked upon our arrival as fulfilling the millennium— the days of "jubilon."

As during the march from Atlanta to Savannah, many blacks abandoned their plantation shanties to follow the army.

Again preserving a wide front, with his columns on roads that were roughly parrallel, Sherman confused the Confederates as to his aims, and they were unable to concentrate against him. At first they believed he would bear to his right and strike Charleston to avenge the capture of Fort Sumter, but he continued northward, knowing that the troops at Charleston would soon evacuate the place out of fear of being cut off.

"The small force in Sherman's front," explains Confederate cavalry, officer J. P. Austin, "offered but slight resistance to his advance. He swept on with his army of sixty thousand men like a full developed cyclone, leaving behind him a track of desolation and ashes...."

Sherman's first objective was Columbia, South Carolina's capital. Reaching Broad River, west of the city, on February 16, his advance troops found the bridge in flames. The next morning, says David Conyngham:

The engineers ... proceeded to lay ... pontoons, while the high bluff on the margin [of the river] was crowded with officers and men. There was General Sherman ... pacing up and down in the midst of the group ... with an unlit cigar in his mouth ... now and then abruptly halting to speak to some of the generals around him. Again he would sit down, whittle a stick, and soon nervously start up to resume his walk....

As soon as the pontoon was laid, General Sherman, accompanied by several other generals, their staffs and orderlies, forming a brilliant cavalcade, rode into the city amidst a scene of the most enthusiastic excitement. Ladies crowded the windows and balconies, waving banners and handkerchiefs. They were the wives and sisters of the few proscribed Union people of Columbia. . . .

Negroes were grouped along the streets, cheering, singing, and dancing in the wild exuberance of their newborn freedom. Perhaps the most flattering compliment paid to us was by a Negro, whom, with upturned features and clasped hands, I heard exclaim, "At last! At last! Our saviours!"

Ringing cheers and shouts [of the soldiers themselves] echoed far and wide, mingled with the martial music of the bands as they played "Hail Columbia," "Yankee Doodle," and other national airs.

Unique among the spectators were numerous Union soldiers who had recently escaped from a nearby prisoner-of-war camp, where they had endured months of misery. One of these men, S. H. M. Byers, slipped up to Sherman as he rode past, handing him a piece of paper that held a song Byers had composed while a prisoner. Entitled "Sherman's March to the Sea," it described the hardships and glories of the campaign, the final verse telling of the arrival before Savannah:

Oh, proud was our army that morning
    That stood where the pine darkly towers,
When Sherman said, "Boys, you are weary,
    But today fair Savannah is ours!"
Then sang we a song of our chieftain
    That echoed o'er river and lea;
And the stars in our banner shone brighter
    When Sherman camped down by the sea!

The song (destined to rise to national fame and to be remembered for generations) pleased Sherman, and he decided to attach its composer to his staff.

The march into Columbia was made in such an orderly way that the citizens believed they might escape serious punishment. But this hope began to wane as Sherman's foragers went to work.

At least one residence, however, got preferential treatment. The story is told by war correspondent De Bow Keim:

While walking through the city . . . the General's quick eye rested upon a peaceful home with fine flocks of chickens and ducks within the inclosure. The lady of the house met him as he entered, the General remarking: "Madame, I am pleased to notice our men have not handled your premises as is their wont."

"I owe it to you, General. . . . You remember our home on Cooper River in 1845? You gave me a book. . . . Here it is."

. . . Turning to the flyleaf, he read: "To Miss Poyas, with the compliments of W. T. Sherman, first lieutenant, Third Artillery."

He instantly recalled the young lady, her fad for water colors, and a mutual sentiment in that direction. He responded with inquiries about her father, mother, and sisters, and particularly her brother . . . with whom he used to hunt on the Cooper, some 40 miles above Charleston.

She told her story. She had heard frightful stories of cruelties and devastations committed along his line of march. . . . So, fortifying herself with this little volume, a long-treasured relic of maiden days, she decided to prayerfully await developments.

The "boys" were on hand and over the fence. In a jiffy the chickens and ducks were scattering in every direction. At length a young man . . . appearing to have authority, entered upon the scene. In womanly desperation, she appealed to him in the name of his general. . . .

"What do you know of Uncle Billy . . .?"

"When he was a young man he was a friend in Charleston, and here is a book he gave me."

. . . The young officer looked it over, shouting: "Hello, boys, here's something!"

The boys, piling over one another to get a squint, sent up a chorus, the officer leading: "That's so. That's Uncle Billy's writing. I have seen it before."

A cessation of hostilities followed. A soldier remained on duty until the provost guard arrived.

"Was the guard good to you?" inquired the General.

"A very nice young man. He is in the other room minding my baby while I have come out to meet you."

Sherman assured Columbia's mayor that he intended to limit his destruction to public buildings and other property useful to the Confederate war effort. But the city wasn't to get off so easily. In the first place,

COLUMBIA in flames.

sparks were already blowing around from cotton stores ignited by the Confederates before Sherman's arrival.

In newsman Conyngham's words:

Towards night, crowds of our escaped prisoners, soldiers, and Negroes intoxicated with their newborn liberty, which they looked upon as license to do as they pleased, were parading the streets in groups.

As soon as night set in, there ensued a sad scene indeed. The suburbs were first set on fire, some assert by the burning cotton.... Pillaging gangs soon fired the heart of the town, then entered the houses, in many instances carrying off articles of value.

The flames soon burst out in all parts of the city, and the streets were quickly crowded with helpless women and children, some in their night clothes....

The scene at the convent was a sad one indeed. The flames were fast encompassing the convent, and the sisters and about sixty terrified young ladies [i.e., schoolgirls] huddled together on the streets. Some of these had come from the North previous to the war, for their education, and were not able to return.

The superioress of the convent had educated General Sherman's daughter Minnie [in Ohio]. He had assigned them a special guard . . . so they felt secure, and were totally unprepared for the dreadful scene that ensued. . . .

I trust I shall never witness such a scene again—drunken soldiers rushing from house to house, emptying them of their valuables and then firing them; Negroes carrying off piles of booty . . . and exulting like so many demons; officers and men revelling on the wines and liquors. . . .

I was fired at for trying to save an unfortunate man from being murdered. . . . Shrieks, groans, and cries of distress resounded from every side. Men, women, and children, some half naked . . . were running frantically about. . . .

True, Generals Sherman, Howard, and others were out giving instructions for putting out a fire in one place, while a hundred fires were lighting all around them. How much better would it have been had they brought in a division or brigade of sober troops and cleared out the town. . . .

The scene continued until near morning, and then the town was cleared out—when there was nothing more to pillage or burn. . . .

Who is to blame for the burning of Columbia is a subject that will be long disputed. I know the Negroes and escaped prisoners were infuriated, and easily incited the inebriated soldiers to join them in their work of vandalism. . . .

The 18th of February dawned upon a city of ruins. . . . The streets were full of rubbish, broken furniture, and groups of crouching, desponding, weeping, helpless women and children. . . .

In one place I saw a lady, richly dressed, with three pretty little children clinging to her. She was sitting on a mattress, while round her were strewn some rich paintings, works of art, and virtu. It was a picture of hopeless misery surrounded by the trappings of refined taste and wealth.

General Sherman ordered six hundred head of cattle and some stores to be left for the nuns and the destitute.

But the Yankees were not yet through with Columbia. As recorded in the diary of aide-de-camp George Nichols on February 19:

General Sherman has given orders for the farther destruction of all public property in the city, excepting the new capital, which will not be injured. I think the General saves this building more because it is such a beautiful work of art than for any other reason.

The arsenal, railroad depots, store-houses, magazines, public property, and cotton to the amount of twenty thousand bales are today destroyed. There is not a rail upon any of the roads within twenty miles of Columbia but will be twisted into corkscrews before the sun sets. . . .

Columbia will have bitter cause to remember the visit of Sherman's army. . . . I know that thousands of South Carolina's sons are in the army of the rebellion; but she has already lost her best blood there. [Many of] those who remain have no homes. . . . The ancient homesteads . . . the heritages of many generations, are swept away.

Upon leaving Columbia, Sherman pursued a northeastward course. His newest staff member, S. H. M. Byers (the songwriter and escaped prisoner), was delighted with his post:

What a change it was, from the degradation, the starving, the suffering . . . to the headquarters of the most brilliant general of modern times.

Sherman was marching . . . in four columns, on as many different roads. . . . One day he would ride with this column, the next day with that. But whenever he appeared among the soldiers it was one loud and continued cheer for "Billy Sherman."

Here was the general whom everybody knew, and whom everybody loved. . . . He was, indeed, looked upon as a sort of common property, in which every man in the army had a special and particular interest. . . . Whenever he appeared, the knapsacks of the boys grew lighter, the step brisk, and the face bright. . . .

It rained nearly all the time. The roads were horrid, and had to be corduroyed with poles and rails half the way. The wagons and the artillery stuck in the mire hourly, and the soldiers had to drag them out with their own hands. Every stream had to be bridged, every quagmire filled, and every mile skirmished with the enemy. . . .

Through all this the boys tugged and fought, and amidst their tugging sang and cheered. It was the magnetism of one really great man. . . . Riding alongside the regiments struggling through the mud or the underbrush . . . he would often speak to the nearest soldiers with some kind and encouraging word. Nor was it unusual to hear private soldiers call out to him. . . .

At headquarters [each evening] there was little pretense and no show. . . . After supper he studied his maps in the firelight, or heard the reports from the other columns for the day. He was last in bed at night, and first in the saddle in the morning. . . .

So the days passed, and the enemy was continually pushed or beaten back from each and every chosen position.

Sherman occupied the town of Cheraw, near the North Carolina border, on March 3. Moving across the border, he took Fayetteville on March 11. Here a large arsenal complex was destroyed.

By this time, Confederate General Joseph Johnston, relieved of his command after failing to thwart Sherman's drive from Chattanooga to Atlanta, had been called up to consolidate all available troops and face him anew. But the task of stopping Sherman was hopeless—particularly since fresh Federals in formidable numbers were moving to join him from a beachhead established near Wilmington, on the North Carolina coast. Contact with these troops had already been established by means of the Cape Fear River.

On March 14 aide-de-camp George Nichols wrote in his diary:

Several transports arrived yesterday from Wilmington, bringing supplies for the army. They returned laden with our sick and wounded soldiers. . . .

We have also taken this opportunity to disencumber the army of the host of Negroes who have joined us day by day. . . . By order of General Sherman, all of these people have been gathered together from the different corps into one camp; and now, under the direction of a competent officer, with a sufficient guard and ample supplies, they are to march to Wilmington. . . .

God help the poor creatures! They have endured exposure and suffering in pursuit of freedom, and they have attained the boon at last.

General Johnston, having managed to assemble an army of about 20,000 men, confronted Sherman near Bentonville on March 19. Fighting continued intermittently until March 21, when Johnston withdrew northward toward Raleigh. Sherman moved eastward to Goldsboro, where the Federals from the coast became a part of his command, raising his total to nearly 90,000 men.

Now less than 200 miles south of Richmond, Sherman was ready to cooperate with General Grant.

◡IX◟

Victory and
the Grand Review

◡*W*ishing *to confer with Grant, Sherman went to the North
Carolina coast and boarded a captured steamer that took him northward
to the mouth of James River, and on up the river toward Grant's
headquarters at City Point. According to Grant's aide, Horace Porter,
the steamer approached the wharf late in the afternoon of March 27,
1865:*

General Grant and two or three of us who were with him at
the time started down to the wharf to greet the Western commander. Before we reached the foot of the steps [that descended the bank to the wharf], Sherman had jumped ashore
and was hurrying forward with long strides to meet his
chief. . . .

Grant cried out, "How d'you do, Sherman!"

"How are you, Grant!" exclaimed Sherman.

And in a moment they stood upon the steps with their hands
locked in a cordial grasp, uttering earnest words of familiar
greeting. Their encounter was more like that of two schoolboys
coming together after a vacation than the meeting of the chief
actors in a great war tragedy.

Sherman walked up with the general-in-chief to headquarters, where Mrs. Grant extended to the illustrious visitor a cordial greeting.

Sherman then seated himself with the others by the campfire, and gave a most graphic description of the stirring events of his march.... Never were listeners more enthusiastic; never was a speaker more eloquent. The story, told as he alone could tell it, was a grand epic related with Homeric power....

After the interview had continued nearly an hour, Grant said to Sherman: "I'm sorry to break up this entertaining conversation, but the President is aboard the *River Queen,* and I know he will be anxious to see you. Suppose we go and pay him a visit before dinner."

"All right," cried Sherman; and the two generals... were soon after seated in the cabin of the steamer with the President.

In about an hour the two commanders came back and entered the general-in-chief's hut. I was there talking to Mrs. Grant at the time. She, with her usual thoughtfulness, had prepared some tea....

"And now let us talk further about the immediate movements of my army," said Sherman.

"Perhaps you don't want me here listening to all your secrets," remarked Mrs. Grant.

"Do you think we can trust her, Grant?" exclaimed Sherman, casting a sly glance at Mrs. Grant.

"I'm not so sure about that, Sherman," said the commander, entering into the spirit of fun....

Sherman laughed... and said: "Now, Mrs. Grant, let me examine you, and I can soon tell whether you are likely to understand our plans well enough to betray them to the enemy."

... Sherman turned his chair squarely toward her, folded his arms... and... proceeded to ask all sorts of geographical questions about the Carolinas and Virginia. Mrs. Grant caught the true essence of the humor.... When asked where a particular river in the South was, she would locate it a thousand miles away.... Railroads and canals were also mixed up in interminable confusion.

She had studied the maps in camp very carefully, and had an excellent knowledge of the geography of the theater of war, and this information stood her in good stead in carrying on the little comedy which was being enacted.

In a short time Sherman turned to his chief, who had been greatly amused by the by-play, and exclaimed: "Well, Grant, I think we can trust her."

And then speaking again to the general's wife, he said: "Never mind, Mrs. Grant; perhaps some day the women will vote and control affairs, and then they will take us men in hand and subject us to worse cross-examinations than that."

... Dinner was now announced, and Sherman escorted Mrs. Grant to the mess-room and occupied a seat beside her at the table.

In the evening several officers came to pay their respects to Sherman. ...

The next morning ... Admiral Porter came to headquarters, and in the course of his conversation said to Sherman: "When you were in the region of those swamps and overflowed rivers ... didn't you wish you had my gunboats with you?"

"Yes," answered Sherman. ... "One day ... while my men were wading a river which was surrounded for miles by swamps ... after they had been in the water for about an hour ... one of them cried out to his chum, 'Say, Tommy, I'm blowed if I don't believe we've struck this river lengthways!'"

After spending a quarter of an hour together, General Grant said that the President was expecting them aboard his boat, and the two generals and the admiral started for the *River Queen*. ...

There now occurred in the upper saloon of that vessel ... [a] conference. ... It was in no sense a council of war, but only an informal interchange of views between the four men who, more than any others, held the destiny of the nation in their hands. ...

Mr. Lincoln asked if it would not be possible to end the matter without a pitched battle, with the attendant losses and suffering; but was informed that that was a matter not within the control of our commanders, and must rest necessarily with the enemy.

Lincoln spoke about the course which he thought had better be pursued after the war, and expressed an inclination to lean toward a generous policy. ...

Sherman related many interesting incidents which occurred in his campaign. Grant talked less than anyone present.

The President twice expressed some apprehension about Sherman being away from his army; but Sherman assured him that he had left matters safe ... and that he would start back ... that day.

That afternoon Sherman took leave of those at headquarters

and returned to his command in the *Bat,* as that vessel was faster than the one which had brought him up the coast.

As it turned out, Sherman and his army did no further fighting. Aided by Sherman's work of the past eleven months, which had helped to sap Lee's strength both materially and morally, Grant and the Army of the Potomac conducted the war's last great campaign. Sherman was just beginning to march against Johnston in North Carolina when he received word that Grant, after driving Lee from Richmond and Petersburg, had obtained his surrender at Appomattox Court House on April 9.

On the fourteenth, Sherman got word from Johnston, by means of a flag of truce, that he wanted to talk terms. Now that the war was drawing to a close, Sherman was prepared to be very generous with the Confederates. He believed that President Lincoln would back him on this. But on April 17, just before he left for a meeting with Johnston near Durham's Station, Sherman learned that Lincoln had been assassinated.

Giving scant consideration to the fact that a new wave of bitterness against the South was sweeping the North, Sherman proceeded as he had planned. The terms he granted Johnston—subject to the approval of Lincoln's successor, Andrew Johnson—were generous indeed, exceeding even Lincoln's concepts. The Confederates, for example, were to be allowed to keep their weapons and take them home for deposit in their state arsenals.

Not stopping with military considerations, Sherman entered civil areas, where he had no authority. The people of the South were to enjoy an immediate return to their rights under the Constitution. Existing state governments, upon the renouncement of their revolutionary aims, were to stay in power.

The terms were signed on April 18, and Sherman at once sent a copy to General Grant, then in Washington. Horace Porter says that Grant recieved the document on April 21:

Perceiving that the terms covered many questions of a civil and not of a military nature, he suggested to the Secretary of War [Edwin Stanton] that the matter had better be referred at once to President Johnson and the cabinet for their action.

A cabinet meeting was called before midnight, and there was a unanimous decision that the basis of the agreement should be disapproved, and an order was issued directing General Grant to proceed in person to Sherman's headquarters. . . .

HOUSE NEAR Durham's Station, North Carolina, within which Sherman and Johnston met to negotiate peace terms. Scene shows Union and Confederate officers discussing the campaign as they await the meeting's outcome.

Instead of merely recognizing that Sherman had made an honest mistake in exceeding his authority, the President and the Secretary of War characterized his conduct as akin to treason, and the Secretary denounced him in unmeasured terms. At this General Grant grew indignant and gave free expression to his opposition to an attempt to stigmatize an officer whose acts throughout all his career gave ample contradiction to the charge that he was actuated by unworthy motives. . . .

Grant started at daybreak on the 22d, proceeded at once to Raleigh, explained the situation and attitude of the government fully to Sherman, and directed him to give the required notice for annulling the truce, and to demand a surrender of Johnston's army on the same terms as those accorded to Lee. [These terms were simple: Lee's men had been deprived of their arms and sent home on parole.]

. . . When [Sherman] went out to the front to meet Johnston, Grant remained quietly in Raleigh . . . lest he might seem to share in the honor of receiving the surrender, the credit for which he wished to belong wholly to Sherman.

Explains Grant himself:

As soon as possible, I started to get away, to leave Sherman quite free and untrammelled. At Goldsboro, on my way back, I met a mail containing the latest newspapers, and I found in them indications of great excitement in the North over the terms Sherman had given Johnston [the furor having been stirred up by public statements made by Secretary Stanton]. . . .

I knew that Sherman must see these papers, and I fully realized what great indignation they would cause him, though I do not think his feelings could have been more excited than were my own. But like the true and loyal soldier that he was he carried out the instructions I had given him, obtained the surrender of Johnston's army, and settled down in his camp about Raleigh to await final orders.

Sherman was soon instructed to bring his army northward to Washington. By May 19 he was encamped near the city's southern outskirts.

I visited the general there [relates Senator John Sherman] and found that he was still smarting under what he called the disgrace put upon him by Stanton. I advised him to keep entirely quiet, said the feeling [against him] had passed away and that his position was perfectly well understood.

I persuaded him to call on the President and such members of the cabinet as he knew, and accompanied him. He was dressed in full uniform, well worn, was bronzed and looked the picture of health and strength. As a matter of course he refused to call on Stanton and denounced him in unmeasured terms, declaring that he would insult him whenever the opportunity occurred.

Sherman had also broken with his old friend General Halleck. The chief of staff, who in an earlier role had sustained Sherman when people were calling him insane, had sided with Stanton against him, taking an equally radical stand. Second thoughts prompted Halleck to write Sherman a letter of apology, but Sherman could not forgive him.

By this time President Johnson had scheduled a grand review of the Eastern and Western armies, prior to their disbandment. According to Horace Porter:

The Army of the Potomac, being senior in date of organization, and having been for four years the more direct defense of

the capital city, was given precedence, and May 23 was designated as the day on which it was to be reviewed. [Sherman's
army was to march on the day after.]

During the preceding five days Washington had been given
over to elaborate preparations for the coming pageant. The
public buildings were decked with a tasteful array of bunting;
flags were unfurled from private dwellings; arches and trans-
parencies with patriotic mottoes were displayed in every quarter; and the spring flowers were fashioned into garlands, and
played their part.

The whole city was ready for the most imposing fete-day in
its history. Vast crowds of citizens had gathered from neighbor-
ing states. During the review they filled the stands, lined the
sidewalks, packed the porches, and covered even the house-
tops. The weather was superb.

A commodious stand had been erected on Pennsylvania Avenue in front of the White House, on which were gathered a
large number of distinguished officials, including the President. . . .

General Grant, accompanied by the principal members of his
staff, was one of the earliest to arrive. . . . Grant's appearance,
was as usual, the signal for a boisterous demonstration. Sherman arrived a few minutes later, and his reception was scarcely
less enthusiastic. [Sherman was joined on the stand by his wife,
his son Tommy, his brother John, and his foster father,
Thomas Ewing, now 75 and having another seven years to live.]

At nine o'clock the signal gun was fired, and the legions [of
the Army of the Potomac] took up their march. They started
from the Capitol, and moved along Pennsylvania Avenue toward Georgetown. . . . Martial music from scores of bands filled
the air, and when familiar war-songs were played the spectators
along the route joined in shouting the chorus. . . .

For nearly seven hours the pageant was watched with un-
abated interest; and when it had faded from view the spectators
were eager for the night to pass, so that on the morrow the
scene might be renewed in the marching of the mighty Army of
the West.

The next day . . . at nine o'clock Sherman's veterans
started. . . . Sherman, unknown by sight to most of the people in
the East, was eagerly watched for, and his appearance [at the
head of the procession] awoke great enthusiasm. His tall, spare

figure, war-worn face, and martial bearing made him all that the people had pictured him.

He had ridden but a little way before his body was decorated with flowery wreaths, and his horse enveloped in garlands. As he approached the reviewing stand the bands struck up "Marching through Georgia," . . . the signal for renewed demonstrations of delight.

When he had passed, he [separated himself from the procession,] turned his horse into the White House grounds, dismounted, and strode rapidly to the platform. He advanced to where the President was standing, and the two shook hands. The members of the cabinet then stepped up to greet him. He took their extended hands, and had a few pleasant words to say to each of them, until Stanton reached out his hand. Then Sherman's whole manner changed in an instant. A cloud of anger overspread his features, and . . . [he] turned abruptly away. This rebuff became the sensation of the day. . . .

Sherman . . . spent all the day in pointing out the different subdivisions of his army as they moved by . . . recalling in his pithy and graphic way many of the incidents of the stirring campaigns through which they had passed. . . .

Each division was preceded by a pioneer corps of Negroes, marching in double ranks, with picks, spades, and axes slung across their brawny shoulders, their stalwart forms conspicuous by their height.

But the impedimenta were the novel feature of the march. Six ambulances followed each division to represent its baggage train; and then came the amusing spectacle of "Sherman's bummers," bearing with them the "spoils of war."

. . . The trophies . . . consisted of pack mules loaded with turkeys, geese, chickens, and bacon, and here and there a chicken-coop strapped on to the saddle, with a cackling brood peering out through the slats. Then came cows, goats, sheep, donkeys, crowing roosters, and in one instance a chattering monkey.

Mixed with these was a procession of fugitive blacks—old men, stalwart women, and grinning pickaninnies of all sizes, ranging in color from a raven's wing to a new saddle. This portion of the column called forth shouts of laughter and continuous rounds of applause. . . .

Comparisons were naturally instituted between the Eastern

and Western armies. . . . The Army of the Potomac presented a somewhat neater appearance . . . and was a little more precise in its movements. Sherman's army showed, perhaps, more of a rough-and-ready aspect and a devil-may-care spirit. . . .

At half past three o'clock the matchless pageant had ceased. For two whole days a nation's heroes had been passing in review. . . . They had made their last march. . . . It was not a Roman triumph, designed to gratify the vanity of the victors, exhibit their trophies, and parade their enchained captives before the multitude. It was a celebration of the dawn of peace, a declaration of the re-establishment of the Union.

The Last
Quarter Century

Since Sherman held a commission in the regular army, he wasn't discharged with the volunteers. But while awaiting new orders he was granted a leave. Among the places he visited was his native Lancaster, Ohio, where he found several thousand people waiting to greet him and to pay him homage. Though he beamed at the greeting, he protested the homage:

I claim no special honor, only to have done a full man's share; for when one's country is in danger, the man who will not defend it and sustain it with his natural strength is no man at all. . . . I have done simply what all the boys in blue have done. I have only labored with the strength of a single man, and have used the brains I inherited and the education given by my country. . . .

The past is now with the historian, but we must still grapple with the future. In this we need a guide, and, fortunately for us all, we can trust the constitution which has safely brought us through the gloom and danger of the past. . . . The Government of the United States and the constitution of our fathers have proven their strength and power in time of war, and I believe our whole country will be even more brilliant in the vast and unknown future than in the past.

It was Sherman's lot to play an important role in the promotion of the national greatness he envisioned. In the summer of 1865 he was placed in command of the Military Division of the Mississippi, his jurisdiction extending across the Great Plains to the Rocky Mountains. In conjunction with his task of dealing with the Indians, Sherman turned special attention to protecting, and assisting with, the construction of the transcontinental railroad that had been chartered by Congress during the war.

Sherman sympathized with the Indians who were being dispossessed and he felt that Congress wasn't sufficiently responsive to their plight, but this did not impede his efforts to subdue them. To the Eastern humanitarians he posed the question "How are you going to settle this great continent from the Atlantic to the Pacific without doing some harm to the Indians who stand in the way?" He told the Indians themselves, "You cannot stop the locomotives any more than you can stop the sun or moon."

Sherman had his headquarters at Saint Louis, Missouri, and for the first time in years he was able to spend some time with his family. Sitting by the fireside, he devoted hours to reading to his children from the works of Charles Dickens, Sir Walter Scott, and Washington Irving.

In January, 1867, Ellen, then in her early forties, gave birth to another boy, Philemon Tecumseh, or "Cumpy, Jr." This completed the family, the surviving children numbering four girls and two boys. Minnie, now fifteen, was the oldest.

Sherman's duties often called him westward across the plains. He saw no fighting, but he enjoyed circulating among the soldiers of the various outposts. According to an officer who accompanied him on one of his tours:

He acted like a boy turned loose—threw off reserve—asked 1,000 questions of everybody—never at a loss for a story or joke—a comic twinkle in his eye—a serio-comic twitch to his wrinkled features—with a long stride he paced up and down constantly, never weary—a prodigious smoker and talker— stretched in blankets before the fire in the shadow of mountains, he talked the night half away.

Hundreds of the civilians engaged in building the railroad were discharged veterans of Sherman's Civil War army, and many still wore their old blue uniforms. As he rode past crews busy laying rails under the wide Western sky, Sherman was often hailed as "Uncle Billy." He laughed with the men over the fact that not long ago they had been associated with railroads in a very different manner.

Sherman had emerged from the war as one of the most influential men in the country, and attempts were made to draw him into national politics, but he preferred to remain strictly a military figure. Repeatedly pressed to accept the post of Secretary of War, he once slipped out from under by volunteering for a minor diplomatic mission to Mexico. His return trip carried him through Jackson, Mississippi, which he had devastated during the Vicksburg campaign, and he was surprised and pleased when many citizens turned out to greet him "in the most friendly spirit."

When Grant became President of the United States in March, 1869, he made Sherman his successor as General of the Army. Sherman was required to move to Washington, and he was there on May 10 when a telegram from the West brought great news about the railroad project. The Union Pacific, running westward from Omaha, Nebraska, and the Central Pacific, running eastward from Sacramento, California, had been joined in a "last spike" ceremony at Promontory, Utah. This was regarded by Sherman as being as important to the nation as the reconstruction of the South, then being stormily effected.

Grant failed to carry his decisiveness as a general into the affairs of the presidency. He had no political acumen, and was easily deceived by scheming subordinates. Corruption began to flourish at all levels of government. Early in Grant's first administration Sherman accepted a temporary appointment as Secretary of War, getting out as soon as he could. Sherman fell into disagreements with Grant over the army's affairs, but the friendship survived.

Sherman disliked his Washington involvements, and he escaped them for ten months in 1871 and 1872 by making an unofficial foreign tour, part of the time accompanied by Grant's son Frederick, a lieutenant of cavalry just out of West Point. Visiting Spain, France, Italy, Egypt, Turkey, Russia, Poland, Austria, Switzerland, Germany, and the British Isles, Sherman was given many entertainments. He hobnobbed with royalty, but also enjoyed mingling with the people in the streets, language barriers notwithstanding.

In Switzerland he spent a week with the American consul general, S. H. M. Byers, formerly one of his staff officers and composer of "Sherman's March to the Sea." Byers was to say later:

I never saw a man so run after by women in my life. When he was leaving a train at Bern a whole crowd of women, old and young, pretty and ugly, children and all, kissed him.

Soon after Sherman returned to Washington, Grant was elected to his second term. This administration was marked by major political and financial scandals. As a result, Sherman's unshakable honesty became all the more admired. According to Washington solon James G. Blaine:

His prestige, after General Grant had retired from the Presidency, was without rival in the country, and there was no national election in which he could not have been easily made the candidate of the Republicans. He had, besides his great fame as a soldier and his stainless character as a man, some peculiar qualities that would have made him not only an available but an irresistible candidate. But to all appeals made to him, he had but one answer. It was a firm negative.

By this time Sherman had written and published his Memoirs. *Both articulate and absorbing, they enjoyed a tremendous sale. At the same time, they were also hotly criticized. Sherman wrote what he believed to be true, but some of his impressions and assessments were at odds with those of other veterans of the war. He knew that this was to be expected, but was disturbed by the charge that he had been unjust to some of his fellow officers. He considered putting out a revised edition, but the plan did not mature.*

While General of the Army, Sherman made periodic visits to West Point. An anecdote of one of these visits is told by William S. Rosecrans, who had attended the institute with Sherman about forty years earlier:

. . . in company with the commandant of cadets, [he] made an inspection tour of the barracks. He wasn't looking for contraband goods, but he got to talking about our old school days at West Point, and he said:

"When I was a cadet, one of the considerations was as to what we were to do with our cooking utensils and other things during our summer vacations, and we used to hide our things in the chimney during the summer months. I wonder if the boys do so still."

This visit was made during the month of June, and when Sherman said this he was in one of the cadets' rooms. As he spoke he went to the fireplace and stuck his cane up the chimney. As he did so, a frying pan, an empty bottle, a suit of citizen's clothes, and a board which had been stretched across the chimney came flying down, and the cadets who occupied the room were thunderstruck.

General Sherman laughed, and telling the commandant not to report the young men, he went to another room.

In 1878 Sherman sustained a major disappointment. He had been counting on his son Tom, recently graduated from Yale, to enter a lucrative profession and be prepared to take over as head of the family, should this become necessary. Now he learned that Tom, with Ellen's blessing, planned to become a Catholic priest.

Through the years, Sherman, casual about religion himself, had yielded to Ellen's wishes concerning Catholic training for the children. Once, when he made a mild protest about her beliefs, she reminded him that he knew she was Catholic when they were married. "Yes," Sherman responded wryly, "but I had no idea you'd get worse!"

Now Sherman protested bitterly, much to Ellen's and Tom's distress. The result was a rift between the pair and Sherman that lasted for many months. Sherman never really accepted Tom's choice, but the family affections were fully restored.

In the summer of 1880 Sherman made an impromptu speech before an assemblage of war veterans and civilians at Columbus, Ohio, in which he said, "There is many a boy here today who looks on war as all glory, but, boys, it is all hell." Soon the whole world was quoting Sherman as having said that "war is hell."

Sherman was sixty-three years old when he retired from the army in 1883. Taking up his home in Saint Louis, he soon began getting letters from Republicans urging him to become their candidate in the next presidential election. He replied with letters of refusal, saying in one:

I have my personal affairs in a state of absolute safety and comfort... and would account myself a fool, a madman, an ass, to embark anew... in a career that may, at any moment, become tempest-tossed by the perfidy, the defalcation, the dishonesty or neglect of any one of a hundred thousand subordinates....

Sherman was still receiving appeals to reconsider when the Republican convention opened in Chicago during the summer of 1884. As a last resort, one of the delegates sent him a telegram. Sherman was home at the time, enjoying a visit from his son Tom, then deeply involved with his training for the priesthood. In Tom's words:

I was at his side in his library... when he received the telegram.... "Your name is the only one we can agree upon. You will have to put aside your prejudices and accept the Presidency."

Without taking his cigar from his mouth, without changing his expression, while I stood there trembling by his side, my father wrote the answer: "I will not accept if nominated and will not serve if elected."

He tossed it over to me to be handed to the messenger, and then went on with the conversation he had been engaged in. In that moment I thought my father a great man.

During the winter of 1884 and spring of 1885, Sherman paid a number of visits to Grant at his home at Mount McGregor, New York. Grant was dying of cancer, at the same time trying to complete his Memoirs. *He won the race with only a few days to spare, dying on July 23. His body was taken, amid elaborate ceremonies in which a saddened Sherman participated, to New York City, where burial was made in Riverside Park.*

According to Hiram Hitchcock, a friend to Sherman and one of the proprietors of the Fifth Avenue Hotel:

After General Grant's funeral was over I spent the evening with General Sherman, and he told me of his plans for the future; that he wanted to move quietly from St. Louis and locate in New York. He said that he thought he should enjoy New York very much, and his youngest son was then finishing his course at Yale, and the change would bring him near to New Haven. . . .

He came here with Mrs. Sherman and the daughters, and the youngest son used to come in frequently from Yale. At his first after-dinner speech in New York—that at the New England Society dinner—General Sherman referred to having moved to New York, and said that he had gone into winter quarters down at the Fifth Avenue Hotel, where there was good grass and water.

The General was very particular to have everything arranged to suit Mrs. Sherman. He said that as to himself it did not make much difference. He was used to roughing it and he could take anything, but he wanted Mrs. Sherman to be very nicely fixed and to have things to her own mind.

On the other hand, Mrs. Sherman said to me: "It doesn't make so very much difference about me, but I wish to have the

General comfortable. Dear old fellow, he has seen a great deal of roughing it, and I want him to be entirely at ease."

... During the General's residence here he was, of course, a conspicuous figure. He was always genial and affable to everyone... and he received and entertained a great many of his old army companions, and aided a vast number of them. In fact, no one knows how many army men General Sherman has, first and last, assisted pecuniarily and in various ways, helping them to get positions and giving them advice and encouragement.

He used to meet hosts of friends and acquaintances in the hotel. I remember his saying once that he would have to stop shaking hands, for he had lost one nail, and if he didn't quit soon he would lose them all. If he went to the dining room, people from different parts of the country who knew him would get up and go over to his table and talk to him. It was a sort of a reception with him all the time—one continuous reception.

Adds New York's famed lawyer, railroad magnate, politician, and orator, Chauncey Depew:

He was at once the most distinguished and delightful figure in our metropolitan society. He seemed to have a most elastic constitution, and endured an amount of social obligation which would have tired out and used up many a younger and stronger man. He loved to be in the company of men and women... and very often he would be found at late suppers, especially theatrical suppers....

I have been with him at hundreds of public dinners, and in studying closely his mental methods and habits of speech, have come to regard him as the readiest and most original talker in the United States. I don't believe that he ever made the slightest preparation, but he absorbed... the spirit of the occasion, and his speech, when he finished, seemed to be as much of a surprise to himself as it was to the audience, and the work of a superior and exceedingly active intelligence....

Sherman's appeal as a speaker was not unqualified. Says another friend, Philadelphia journalist A. K. McClure, "He was incapable of dissembling, and often blurted out the truth as he accepted it in a way that was not always acceptable to his hearers."

SHERMAN at sixty-eight.

Ellen shared but few of her husband's social activities, preferring to spend as much time as she could working for the church. She once said, "I owe the public nothing, and am nothing to the public." She was delighted when, in late summer, 1888, Cump established her in a new home at 75 West Seventy-first Street. But she had little time to enjoy it, dying of heart disease on November 28. She was sixty-four.

Sherman, now sixty-eight, was plunged into the deepest gloom, and for weeks it seemed that his own health must fail. He lost weight, and his asthma became severe. For long hours at a time he sat alone, refusing the solace of his children and the many others who offered it.

But the beginning of the year 1889 found Sherman improved in both mind and body. He turned to answering his correspondence, which was always heavy, and he resumed a busy social life, patronizing the theater, speaking at dinners, journeying to veterans' reunions, visiting in the Catskill Mountains.

One man who met him for the first time at a gathering in the Catskills says that Sherman gave the appearance of being "without the slightest trace of vanity or egotism."

He seemed as natural, as warm-hearted, and as simple as a child . . . greeted everybody with cordiality, and made us feel at ease in his company. . . . When offered some refreshment . . . he raised his glass and, glancing around, said, "Gentlemen, in the famous words of John Phenix, I impair my own health by drinking yours." ... He told many interesting anecdotes of famous men whom he met—Lincoln, Grant, Von Moltke, Bismarck, and others.

With the abatement of his grief, Sherman settled into a kind of sunset content. Explains Grant's former aide, Horace Porter:

In whatever circle he moved, he was the center; at whatever table he sat, he was the head. The nation had lifted him to the highest military rank; Congress had presented him with votes of thanks; universities and colleges had conferred on him the degree of LL.D.; numberless home and foreign clubs and societies had made him an honorary member. There were no more public honors to bestow, and now he was receiving the courtesies and attentions of private life in a manner which gave the sweetest solace to the veteran's declining years.

As the year 1890 ended, Sherman had a presentiment that his own end was near, telling a friend, "I feel it coming sometimes when I get home from an entertainment or banquet, especially these winter nights. I feel death reaching out for me, as it were. I suppose I'll take cold some night and go to bed, never to get up again."

It happened very nearly as he predicted. The cold seized him on February 5, 1891, soon to be complicated by facial erysipelas (an acute inflammation of the skin) and asthma. On his seventy-first birthday, February 8, two physicians were summoned. For six more days he lay, while murmuring groups milled about on the street in front of his house, and while telegrams kept the nation and the world informed of his condition. He died of pneumonia on February 14.

The military funeral, which began at the house, was attended by President Benjamin Harrison and scores of other notables, including Sherman's former enemy, Joseph Johnston. The raw weather was hard on the eighty-four-year-old Southerner, who stood on the sidewalk with his head bared as the flag-draped casket was brought out the front door. He himself was to die of pneumonia a month later.

The great procession of carriages and mourners on foot passed through the crowd-lined streets to the train that had been prepared to carry the body to Saint Louis, Missouri. Among the people who gathered along the rail route from New York to Saint Louis to watch the train pass were groups of Civil War veterans, many of them Sherman's own

SCENE OUTSIDE Sherman's house during his last hours.

men. *They held up tattered battle flags, fired salutes with old army muskets, and stood with moist eyes as the train vanished in the distance.*

At Calvary Cemetery in Saint Louis, Father Tom Sherman consigned the casket to the soil. An honor guard fired three rifle volleys, a bugler blew the sad strains of "taps," and the mourners drifted away.

With Ellen and Sergeant Willie beside him, William Tecumseh Sherman was at rest.

Bibliography

Annals of the War. Philadelphia: The Times Publishing Company, 1879.

Austin, J. P. *The Blue and the Gray.* Atlanta: The Franklin Printing and Publishing Co., 1899.

Barrett, John G. *Sherman's March Through the Carolinas.* Chapel Hill, N. C.: The University of North Carolina Press, 1956.

Battles and Leaders of the Civil War. 4 vols. Robert Underwood Johnson and Clarence Clough Buel (eds.). New York: The Century Co., 1884–1888.

Bowman, S. M., and Irwin, R. B. *Sherman and His Campaigns.* New York: Charles B. Richardson, 1865.

Boynton, H. V. *Sherman's Historical Raid: The Memoirs in the Light of the Record.* Cincinnati: Wilstach, Baldwin & Co., 1875.

Browne, Junius Henri. *Four Years in Secessia.* Hartford: O. D. Case and Company, 1865.

Chase, Edward. *The Memorial Life of General William Tecumseh Sherman.* Chicago: R. S. Peale & Co., 1891.

Chesnut, Mary Boykin. *A Diary from Dixie.* New York: D. Appleton & Co., 1905.

Cist, Henry M. *The Army of the Cumberland* (Campaigns of the Civil War, vol. 7). New York: Charles Scribner's Sons, 1882.

Civil War Naval Chronology. Compiled by Naval History Division, Navy Department. Washington, D. C.: Government Printing Office, 1971.

Coffin, Charles Carleton. *The Boys of '61.* Boston: Estes and Lauriat, 1884.

Commager, Henry Steele. *The Blue and the Gray.* Indianapolis and New York: The Bobbs-Merrill Company, Inc., 1950.

Conyngham, David P. *Sherman's March Through the South.* New York: Sheldon and Company, 1865.

Coppée, Henry. *Grant and His Campaigns.* New York: Charles B. Richardson, 1866.

Cox, Jacob D. *Atlanta* (Campaigns of the Civil War, vol. 9). New York: Charles Scribner's Sons, 1882.

————. *The March to the Sea: Franklin and Nashville* (Campaigns of the Civil War, vol. 10). New York: Charles Scribner's Sons, 1882.

Dana, Charles A. *Recollections of the Civil War*. New York: D. Appleton and Company, 1898.

————. *The Life of Ulysses S. Grant*. Springfield, Mass.: Gurdon Bill & Company, 1868.

Dillahunty, Albert. *Shiloh;* Historical Handbook No. 10. Washington, D. C.: Government Printing Office, 1961.

Everhart, William C. *Vicksburg:* Historical Handbook No. 21. Washington, D. C.: Government Printing Office, 1961.

Fiske, John. *The Mississippi Valley in the Civil War*. Boston and New York: Houghton, Mifflin and Company, 1900.

Fletcher, Thomas C. *Life and Reminiscences of Gen. Wm. T. Sherman by Distinguished Men of His Time*. Lenox Publishing Company, 1891.

Force, M. F. *From Fort Henry to Corinth* (Campaigns of the Civil War, vol. 2). New York: Charles Scribner's Sons, 1881.

Garland, Hamlin. *Ulysses S. Grant: His Life and Character*. New York: Doubleday & McClure Co., 1898.

Grant, U. S. *Personal Memoirs*. New York: Charles L. Webster & Company, 1894.

Greeley, Horace. *The American Conflict*. 2 vols. Hartford: O. D. Case & Company, 1864, 1867.

Greene, Francis Vinton. *The Mississippi* (Campaigns of the Civil War, vol. 8). New York: Charles Scribner's Sons, 1882.

Guernsey, Alfred H., and Alden, Henry M. *Harper's Pictorial History of the Great Rebellion*. 2 vols. Chicago: McDonnell Bros., 1866, 1868.

Hansen, Harry. *The Civil War*. New York: Bonanza Books, 1962.

Harper's Encyclopedia of United States History. 10 vols. New York: Harper & Brothers, 1915.

Headley, P. C. *Facing the Enemy: The Life and Military Career of Gen. William Tecumseh Sherman*. Boston: Lee and Shepard, 1865.

Hedley, F. Y. *Marching Through Georgia*. Chicago: M. A. Donohue & Co., 1884.

Hoehling, A. A. *Vicksburg: 47 Days of Siege*. Englewood Cliffs, N. J.: Prentice-Hall, Inc., 1969.

Johnson, Rossiter. *Campfires and Battlefields*. New York: The Civil War Press, 1967.

Johnson, W. Fletcher. *Life of Wm. Tecumseh Sherman*. Edgewood Publishing Company, 1891.

Jones, Katharine M. *When Sherman Came: Southern Women and the "Great March."* Indianapolis, Kansas City, New York: The Bobbs-Merrill Company, Inc., 1964.

Keim, DeB. Randolph. *Sherman: A Memorial in Art, Oratory, and Literature by the Society of the Army of the Tennessee, with the aid of the Congress of the United States of America*. Washington, D. C.: Government Printing Office, 1904.

King, W. C., and Derby, W. P. *Campfire Sketches and Battlefield Echoes of the Rebellion*. Springfield, Mass.: W. C. King & Co., 1887.

Larke, Julian K. *General Grant and His Campaigns*. New York: J. C. Derby & N. C. Miller, 1864.

Lewis, Lloyd. *Sherman: Fighting Prophet.* New York: Harcourt, Brace and Company, 1932.

Long, E. B., (with Barbara Long). *The Civil War Day by Day.* Garden City, N. Y.: Doubleday & Company, Inc., 1971.

Lossing, Benson J. *Pictorial Field Book of the Civil War.* 3 vols. New York: T. Belknap & Company, 1868.

Lusk, William Thompson. *War Letters.* New York: Privately printed, 1911.

McClure, Alexander K. *Recollections of Half a Century.* Salem, Mass.: The Salem Press Company, 1902.

Merrill, James M. *William Tecumseh Sherman.* Chicago, New York, San Francisco: Rand McNally & Company, 1971.

Mitchell, Joseph B. *Decisive Battles of the Civil War.* New York: G. P. Putnam's Sons, 1955.

Moore, Frank, (ed.). *The Civil War in Song and Story.* New York: P. F. Collier, 1889.

————. *The Rebellion Record.* 12 vols. New York: G. P. Putnam, 1861–1871.

Nichols, George Ward. *The Story of the Great March.* New York: Harper & Brothers, 1865.

Northrop, Henry Davenport. *Life and Deeds of General Sherman.* Waukesha, Wis.: World Publishing Co., 1891.

Porter, David D. *Incidents and Anecdotes of the Civil War.* New York: D. Appleton and Company, 1886.

Porter, Horace. *Campaigning with Grant.* New York: The Century Company, 1897.

Richardson, Albert D. *A Personal History of Ulysses S. Grant.* Hartford: American Publishing Company, 1868.

Robins, Edward. *William T. Sherman.* Philadelphia: George W. Jacobs & Company, 1905.

Senour, F. *Major General William T. Sherman and His Campaigns.* Chicago: Henry M. Sherwood, 1865.

Sherman, John. *Recollections of Forty Years in the House, Senate and Cabinet.* 2 vols. Chicago, New York, London and Berlin: The Werner Company, 1895.

Sherman, William T. *Memoirs:* 2 vols. New York: D. Appleton and Company, 1875.

Stowe, Harriet Beecher. *Men of Our Times.* Hartford: Hartford Publishing Co., 1868.

Tarbell, Ida M. *The Life of Abraham Lincoln.* 2 vols. New York: McClure, Phillips & Co., 1902.

Under Both Flags: A Panorama of the Great Civil War. Chicago: W. S. Reeve Publishing Co., 1896.

Vilas, William Freeman. *A View of the Vicksburg Campaign.* Wisconsin History Commission, 1908.

Williams, T. Harry. *Lincoln and His Generals.* New York: Alfred A. Knopf, Inc., 1952.

Wilson, James Grant, and Coan, Titus Munson. *Personal Recollections of the War of the Rebellion.* New York: New York Commandery, 1891.

Young, Jesse Bowman. *What a Boy Saw in the Army.* New York: Hunt & Eaton, 1894.

Index